*A Message
to the
Charismatic
Movement*

A Message to the Charismatic Movement

Larry Christenson

DIMENSION BOOKS
Bethany Fellowship, Inc.
Minneapolis, Minnesota

Dedication

To that body of Christians
Little known of men
But known of God,
Whose message speaks to us
Across the years.

A WORD OF THANKS

This book represents part of the research which the author did while in residence as a Fellow at the Institute for Ecumenical and Cultural Research, St. John's Abbey and University, Collegeville, Minnesota, 1971-72. The author wishes to express his deep appreciation to Father Kilian McDonnell, O.S.B., director of the Institute; Dr. Calvin J. Eichhorst, assistant director; and Sister Helen Peddle, secretary; and also to the other Fellows of the Institute during my year of residence, all of whom helped to make both pleasant and profitable my year of study and reflection on the meaning of the charismatic movement for the Church today. And a very special word of thanks to my congregation, Trinity Lutheran Church, San Pedro, California, which generously granted me a sabbatical leave to undertake this year of research and writing.

Pentecost, 1972   Larry Christenson

CONTENTS

Chapter   Page

1. Charismatic Panorama   11

2. Forgotten Forerunner of the
   Charismatic Movement   15

3. "Renew Your Wonders in
   Our Time . . ."   19

4. Edward Irving: Presbyterian Pioneer   32

5. The Church: The Body of Christ   41

6. The Baptism with the Holy Spirit   55

7. Unity in the Body of Christ   73

8. Ministry in the Body of Christ   87

9. Authority in the Body of Christ   93

10. "Unless a Seed Fall into the Ground
    and Die . . ."   108

Notes: 113

CHAPTER ONE

Charismatic Panorama

A small group of people gathers for weekly prayer in the home of a prominent lawyer. In the course of the evening, the hostess, a woman of quiet disposition, speaks three sentences in an unknown tongue, then three sentences in English: "The Lord will speak to His people! The Lord hasteneth His Coming! The Lord cometh! He cometh! He cometh!" When this development is reported to their pastor, a bitter polemic is launched from the pulpit against the 'gifts.' The family stays on in the congregation for a time, but finally decides to seek spiritual fellowship elsewhere. . .

A young woman lies near death. The doctors have given her but a few days to live. She speaks to her brother for some time, about spiritual things, and concludes with a solemn prayer that he might at that time be endowed with the power of the Holy Ghost. Almost instantly the brother calmly says, "I have got it." He walks to the window and stands silent for a minute or two. Then, with a step and manner of most indescribable majesty, he walks to his sister's bedside, takes her by the hand, and says, "Arise, and stand upright." The young woman stands up, healthy and strong. News of the healing travels far and wide. . .

A Roman Catholic priest begins to hold cottage prayer meetings in his parish. Two people speak out in prophecy: "The Judge stands at the door. Christ will soon appear. . . ." "I will again send you apostles and prophets, as at the beginning, and I will pour out my Spirit. . . ." The priest encounters some difficulties with his superiors. . .

A Presbyterian minister is put out of his church for allowing the manifestation of spiritual gifts in the Sunday service. An Anglican priest declares that charismatic manifestations are of the devil. A wealthy businessman withdraws from his congregation, and begins to hold prayer meetings in his own home . . .

Suddenly young people take to the streets, witnessing and preaching—in parks, public buildings, open places—wherever they find someone to listen. They cheerfully put up with insults, police questioning, bellows of derision. Newspapers call them fanatics . . .

Churches which welcome charismatic manifestations draw large crowds of visitors, but they do little proselyting; most of the visitors return to their own churches, often witnessing about these manifestations to their fellow members. The gifts of the Holy Spirit, long the province of dry theological commentaries, suddenly excite wide public interest. A spate of publications pour out of the press: personal testimonies, ecclesiastical advice, theological opinion. Churches with a long history of placid decorum are suddenly summoned by their officials to man the ramparts against the tides of fanaticism.

One loses count of the theories and explanations for glossalalia, the technical name for speaking in tongues. Three linguists analyze a sample of tongues speech and conclude that it is no language or dialect with which they are familiar. A minister, who himself does not speak in tongues, declares that he nevertheless believes it to be of God, and that it appears to open up new dimensions of worship.

The practice of 'tithing,' giving the first tenth of one's income to the church, begins to be widely practiced by those who practice or profess a belief in the spiritual gifts, arousing some interest, but no real opposition. . . . Those who participate in the move-

13

ment seem to come from all levels of society, though the leaders are distinctly middle and upper class men of culture, education, and of some social importance. Some church leaders denounce the movement openly. Some seek to dispose of it quietly, by removing a minister who may be promoting it. Others allow it a limited, if somewhat uneasy, acceptance.

Any person with a measure of experience in the present-day charismatic movement would have little trouble supplying names, dates, and places for the events we have just described, add or subtract a detail or two. And, indeed, the events are real; historically verifiable.[1] But they did not take place in the 1960's or 1970's. They took place around 1830, in England, Scotland, and Germany. Later the movement spread to other countries in Europe, and to North America. It came to be known as the Catholic Apostolic Church.

14

CHAPTER TWO

Forgotten Forerunner of the Charismatic Movement

The Catholic Apostolic Church appears to have had no direct influence upon the present-day charismatic or neo-Pentecostal movement. Yet its history, its teachings, its theological stance, its concerns—in a word, its *message*, seen as an organic whole —bears striking resemblances to the charismatic movement.

The charismatic movement offers a new point-of-reference, a historical analogy and comparison, for a fresh understanding of the Catholic Apostolic Church.[2] This in itself is not unimportant. The Catholic Apostolic Church has represented something of an enigma to churchmen, rather like "a beautiful Church built from the roof downwards, coming down from above, like New Jerusalem," as one Anglo-Catholic cleric has rather quaintly put it.[3] It was in essence—and this is its most striking feature—a revival of Catholicism out of

15

Protestantism.[4] It was described by an influential writer of the day as "answering to the great religious desideratum of the age—a simple creed, a gorgeous ritual, and a devoted priesthood."[5] Its liturgy is incomparable, described by Dr. David Hislop, in his Kerr Lectures, as "containing all the virtues and escaping all the blemishes of the Book of Common Prayer."[6] Its Book of Regulations describes a quality of spiritual nurture and care for its members which could well serve as a primer in Pastoral Theology. It founded churches throughout Europe and America, and produced a not insignificant literature. Yet it is, today, almost totally unknown in Christendom. And where it is known, it is most often misunderstood. The charismatic movement offers us a perspective and a parallel for positively evaluating the message of its forgotten forerunner.

Secondly, and more important, the Catholic Apostolic Church offers a historical perspective for evaluating the charismatic movement. Many of the questions which are being raised by and in the charismatic movement were also questions which the Catholic Apostolic Church had to face. One of the recurrent themes which one encounters in the self-understanding of the Catholic Apostolic Church is the con-

16

viction that it was to experience certain things not only for itself, but on behalf of the Church as a whole.[7] (An ecumenical vision and spirit characterized virtually every aspect of its history and teaching.[8]) *It is our purpose to look at some of the elements which make up the message of the Catholic Apostolic Church, and to consider their value for the Church today.*

The literature of the Catholic Apostolic Church is voluminous, though quite difficult to come by, as most of it is out of print. A partial bibliography compiled in 1908 lists over 3000 separate titles.[9] They dealt with the whole spectrum of Christian doctrine, elaborating a coherent theological system. We will not attempt even to summarize this large body of teaching, other than to say that it is essentially an expression of the orthodox and historic faith of the ecumenical creeds.

Our approach, rather, will be to touch on some doctrines which have a particular relevance to the charismatic movement. We will seek to illustrate the relevance and practical application of these teachings for the Church today, especially in relation to her experience with the charismatic movement since 1960. In this, we will not attempt to compose a comprehensive picture of the charismatic movement, but rather will draw principally from the experience of and within our own congregation, Trinity Lutheran Church, San Pedro, California.

While this approach presents fewer possibilities for broad generalization (for each congregation and each situation is somewhat unique), it offers the advantage of more concrete analysis in terms of 1) *continuity*, i.e., seeing certain principles put into practice over a sufficiently long span of time, and with the same group of people, to judge their 'staying power,' their long-term effect; 2) *relatedness*, i.e., seeing how certain perhaps new emphases are able to relate in a wholesome way to the whole corpus of Christian truth and life embodied in a particular historical tradition.

CHAPTER THREE

"Renew Your Wonders in Our Time . . ."

We tend to date historical movements from a particular event through which the movement 'surfaces,' an event which embodies some essential characteristic of the movement, and which somehow catalyzes a milieu which has become ripe for that which the event comes to symbolize. Thus we date the Reformation from Luther's nailing of the 95 Theses, the Methodist movement from Wesley's Aldersgate experience, the Pentecostal movement from the revival at the Azusa Street Mission in Los Angeles in 1906; the charismatic movement is usually dated from the outbreak of speaking in tongues at St. Mark's Episcopal Church in Van Nuys, California, in 1960.[10]

The movement which eventually took the form of the Catholic Apostolic Church may be dated, significantly, from the first day of spring—March 21, 1830. On that day a pious, uneducated girl named Mary Campbell lay close to death in Fernicarry, Scotland. For weeks she had been unable even to sit up in bed. Suddenly she raised up, stood out of bed, and began to speak melodiously in an unknown tongue, and to prophesy. She continued for a quarter of an hour, then returned to her bed in former weakness. Word of this event spread, and not long afterward similar occurrences took place in the MacDonald home in Port Glasgow, a few miles distant. Margaret MacDonald, also lying on her deathbed, was healed at the command of her brother James. On that same day, James wrote a letter to Mary Campbell encouraging her, also, to 'stand up and walk.' Upon reading the letter, Mary rose up from her bed well, and walked to Port Glasgow to meet the MacDonalds.[11]

Word of these events stirred great interest, both in Scotland and in England. Men from London, who had long prayed for an outpouring of the Holy Spirit, sent several of their number to Scotland to investigate. They returned convinced that what they had seen and heard was a true work of the Holy Spirit. They established meetings in various houses to pray for a restoration of the spiritual gifts. About a year later, on April 30, 1831, the first manifestation took place in London: Mrs. John Cardale, wife of a prominent Anglican lawyer, spoke in tongues.[12] During the course of that year, tongues and prophecy were experienced by several other persons, from various religious denominations These manifestations, accompanied by a number of healings, continued to increase and spread throughout 1832.[13]

The present-day charismatic movement began similarly, with an experience of the Holy Spirit which manifested itself charismatically—speaking in tongues, prophecy, vision; also, to some extent, an emphasis on healing and exorcism, though this had been developing as a separate stream in many of the historic churches during the preceding decades.

The keynote of the charismatic movement may well have been struck by Pope John XXIII, in the prayer with which he concluded his convocation of the Second Vatican Council, in 1961: "Renew Your wonders in our time, as though for a new Pentecost. . . ." [14] It is this 'new Pentecost,' a great outpouring of the Holy Spirit, which has become the focus of expectation in the charismatic movement.

A note of expectancy appears to be one of the characteristics of charismatic Christianity. It was a marked feature of the

Catholic Apostolic Church: They expected God to speak and act in everyday situations. And one sees a clear parallel to this in the present-day charismatic movement. Indeed, it might be sensibly argued that one of the most distinguishing marks of the charismatic movement is just this: *the focus of its expectation*. People expect *God* to act; the charismatic dimension has alerted them to the fact that God is both *real* and *active*. They begin to take spiritual things more seriously, not out of a sense of duty, but out of this sense of expectancy. The charismatic has introduced a new element into their framework of belief, what Emil Brunner calls, "the 'pneumatic factor,' the non-theological, the purely dynamic. Outsiders," says Brunner, "were attracted—the story of Pentecost already shows us this quite plainly—not primarily by what was said, but by the element of mystery—what happened simply. The impression made by the life of believers plays a decisive part in the genesis of faith. People draw near the Christian community because they are irresistibly attracted by its supernatural power. They would like to share in this new dimension of life and power . . . there is a sort of fascination which is exercised mostly without any reference to the Word, comparable rather to

22

the attractive force of a magnet or the spread of an infectious disease." [15]

The charismatic movement thus offers to a parish one of the basic raw materials for spiritual power and renewal: People whose faith in the living God has been quickened, people who reckon seriously upon the 'wonders of God' in everday life.

This sense of expectancy does not necessarily begin with anything particularly dramatic. The first thing we noticed in our congregation, among people who entered into this experience, was simply a deepened interest in spiritual things: They prayed, read their Bibles, and witnessed to their faith. More-or-less spontaneously, they began to do the things which the Church had always been telling them they ought to do.

Dennis Bennett, the minister in whose parish the charismatic movement is considered to have begun, tells of the initial coolness which he felt toward the ministry while he was growing up, because his clergyman father seemed to spend 95% of his time at the thankless task of "trying to convince people to become interested in God." The charismatic movement has dramatically changed that situation in Bennett's own present parish, St. Luke's Episcopal, Seattle, Washington. Our experience in San Pedro has been similar. Much less effort is required to crank up the machinery and keep it running. We do many of the same things, but this sense of expectation in the charismatic movement, while it surely does not dispense with human planning and effort, often gives it a decidedly new twist—just because of this 'pneumatic factor,' this expectation that God is going to take a hand in things.

About 1968 it became evident to us that we needed larger facilities to accommodate our growing youth program. Ninety children were crowded into a small parish hall every Wednesday evening, while we had to borrow the facilities of the local synagogue to accommodate a group of 30-40 teenagers.

We talked and prayed about it for over a year. As early as 1964, we had had some experience of answered prayer in regard to finances. Seven men had met every week to pray for some projects which we felt we should undertake, but for which we had no money. About $13,000 came in, over and above the budget, and we were able to do about a third of the projects we had been praying for. But this which now faced us was much bigger. The kind of building which we needed would cost about $100,000 —a large amount for our congregation of 200 adult members.

By the spring of 1969 we felt it was time to get under way. We had, however, two unresolved questions: 1) *When should we begin?* A Building Fund Drive started in the late spring would probably run on into the summer. It might be wiser to wait until the fall, when people get back from vacations. 2) *How should we do it?* The thought had come to us that maybe God wanted to do something altogether different. Maybe He wanted to 'visit' people himself, in His own way. We would simply show the kind of building we needed, and then let people respond as God moved them. "We won't call you, you call us." It seemed a little extreme.

On a Friday morning in June, as I came into my study, I saw a brown manila envelope lying on the floor, below the mail slot. I opened it up, and the first thing that caught my eye was a $1000 bill. Then another, and another—five in all. And bundles of $100 bills. I dumped the contents onto my desk and counted out $25,000. There was no identification on the envelope, only a Bible notation. (To this day we haven't the slightest idea where it came from.) I read the Bible passage which was written on the envelope, 2 Corinthians 6. A verse at the beginning, and a verse at the end of that chapter seemed to speak to the questions which we had been pondering: 1) *When should we begin?* "Behold, now is the acceptable time." 2) *How should we do it?* "God said, 'I will live in them and move among them, and I will be their God, and they shall be my people.'"

We followed this leading. There was no formal fund raising. We began to build before the full amount was in hand. The prayer continued, and quite a sense of adventure developed. Sometimes gifts came in just a day or two before money was needed to meet a payment with the contractor. No payment was missed, or even late. When the building was dedicated, a wonderful sense of joy *in what God had done* pervaded the congregation. When congratulations go to men, there is approval, admiration, and a sense of gratitude, which is certainly not bad in itself. But when the glory focuses upon what *God* has done, then there is an outbreak of sheer joy, in which *everyone* shares.

The Catholic Apostolic Church distinguished between a 'natural work' and a 'spiritual work.' A work which is initiated and wrought in the Spirit will endure. It has eternal value. A Spirit-initiated work is something which God has prepared beforehand (Eph. 2:10). He has designed it as an occasion through which, during which, something of Christ may be formed in an individual or group. Such a work, therefore, does not only bring blessing here and now; its value lasts into eternity. It is not "burned up" (1 Cor. 3:15). By contrast, a work initiated and wrought purely in the power of human imagination and resource, may meet an immediate, outward need. But the inner need, the eternal dimension of having Christ formed in us while we 'walk in the work,' will be missing. The kind of works, the kind of situations and callings by which Christ may be formed in a given person at a given time are simply too diverse, too subtle, too 'impossible' for human wisdom to devise or to comprehend. This is Paul's basic argument in the first part of his epistle to the Church at Corinth: "The world does not know God through wisdom. . . . God has made foolish the wisdom of the world." A work which is initiated and wrought purely in the power of human wisdom, not having been prepared beforehand by God, will lack the necessary configuration of human and divine factors by which the Holy Spirit is able to bring a person or a group to that particular encounter with the living Christ which God, in His wisdom, knows they are now able to profit from and assimilate.

The new building stands on our church

property as a testimony to a specific dealing of God with us as a people. It testifies to a God who involves himself in the lives of His people in specific and unthought-of ways. The gifts of the Holy Spirit—in this particular case, prophecy, miracle, revelation, faith—are real. God uses them to accomplish His purposes in concrete situations. This is a basic thrust of the charismatic movement, which God illustrated to us in this experience.

It needs to be noted, *emphatically noted*, that God was not showing us a "new stewardship method," in the sense of a technique which we could apply mechanically to future situations. That would miss the whole point, which is the *creative initiative of God*. In another situation, He might direct us to enter into a perfectly conventional fund-raising drive. Or, more likely (for His creative work is developmental, cumulative), building upon this experience of faith, He would lead us into a work wherein we would be called to trust Him in yet further, undreamed-of ways. And this does not at all mean ways which are more 'ethereal,' or 'impractical.'

When Bethany Fellowship, a community for the training and support of missionaries, first began to manufacture camping trailers, they had no idea what kind of a market

28

they would find for such a product. They received a word of prophecy that they should build 48 trailers the first year. It was an untried market, and that was exactly the number which they were able to sell. When they prayed about it the next year, the Lord told them, quite simply, "Use the common sense I've given you." That word has stood them in good stead ever since; the market has expanded, and they are able to sell all they make. It is not new methods and techniques which God is offering the Church through the charismatic movement, but rather a new confidence that *He will act.*

When we first heard of God's miracles among other groups, we tried to 'copy' them. Sometimes it worked, sometimes not; God was teaching us, patiently, and like a good Teacher, He knows that we need encouragement along the way, even when we are somewhat off target. Little by little we came to see that a testimony of God's miracles has one proper purpose: to point us to God Himself, to glorify Him, to encourage us to trust Him.

We continued to hear the testimonies of other persons and groups in the charismatic movement. But our response changed. Instead of jumping on the Enthusiasm Bandwagon with a hearty, "Let's try it!", we began to gather quietly before God with prayers something like this: "What a wonderful thing You have done *there*, Lord. Now . . . what do You want to do *here?*" The answer to such a prayer, in its outward form, might bear but slight resemblance to the work of God somewhere else which actually inspired it. The unity is found not in the outward form of the ministry, but in the inner dynamic: "There are varieties of working, but the same God" (1 Cor. 12:6). Churches in a given denomination may have the same 'program,' utilize the same 'techniques,' yet experience little sense of unity with one another. When God, through the working and gifts of His Holy Spirit, more and more initiates and empowers our programs, we will see in a cross-section of congregations a scintillating variety; yet, underneath, we will sense an almost awe-inspiring unity . . . for it is *God* who has done it.

The charismatic happenings in England ignored denominational boundaries. From 1830-1833, the movement located in churches or home groups wherever a clergyman or influential layman had stepped out to embrace the new phenomena: an Anglican parish in Albury, an independent congregation in Bishopsgate, a non-denominational fellowship in Southwark, an Anglican parish in Park-Chapel, a Baptist congregation in Oxford. And in Scotland, people gathered together in home groups, or in churches, to share a fellowship and a freedom in worship which stirred the dour Scotch religious temperament like a bracing wind. In southern Germany, somewhat earlier than the events in Scotland, there had been tongues and prophesying in a Roman Catholic parish, which later made contact with the movement in England. [16]

Though the movement was diffuse, growing spontaneously without organization or direction, it came to a certain focus in the public mind in the person of the minister of the National Scottish Church in Regent Square, London, the most famous preacher of his day, Edward Irving.

CHAPTER FOUR

Edward Irving:
Presbyterian Pioneer

The name of Edward Irving is inextricably linked with the history and development of the Catholic Apostolic Church. Adherents to the movement were dubbed "Irvingites," a designation which Irving himself protested bitterly. [17] Yet to this day, "Irvingism" is the convenient handle by which many people dispose of the movement, often in a pejorative sense, as when foreigners dispose of all Americans with the designation "Yankee." The fact of the matter is that the name of Edward Irving, for all the notability which it enjoyed during his own lifetime, is today little more than a name to most students of church history, somewhat vaguely identified with speaking in tongues, prophecy, and other sundry fanaticisms.

How far this is from an accurate estimate of the man, and his ministry, may be discovered by the most cursory reading of his life. Irving had arrived in London in 1822, unknown, newly ordained, to minister to a handful of Scotsmen at the little Caledonian Chapel in Hatton Garden. In a matter of months that little chapel had become the center of attraction in the great metropolis. High society and low flocked to hear the Scotsman preach, rather smitten than deterred by three-hour long services, and thundering denunciations of their irreligion and immorality. Orators, scholars, and nobles hung upon his lips, as he discoursed of righteousness, temperance, and judgment to come, with the boldness and power of one of the old prophets. [18] Within two years, the congregations had outgrown the tiny chapel, and a large new church was built in Regent Square.

Yet, impressive as was his power in the pulpit, Irving's gifts as a pastor—a shepherd of souls—were more impressive still, and stood somewhat in contrast to his flamboyant oratorical style. Before ordination, he had worked as an assistant to the great Rev. Chalmers; in the slums of Glasgow, he acquired a life-long sympathy, rapport, and pastoral concern for the 'simple poor of the earth.' When fame visited upon him the adulation of the mighty, with ever-increasing demands upon his time; and later, when storm clouds of controversy lowered about him, he never ceased his quiet and faithful shepherding of the flock entrusted to his care. [19] He was, above all, a man in whom a humble sense of calling took precedence over all else which the world might direct toward him, for good or for ill. The poet Samuel Coleridge wrote of him: "He is a mighty contender for spiritual religion and true evangelical piety, in whom I see, more than in any of his contemporaries, the spirit of Luther." [20] "He was," wrote Thomas Carlyle after Irving's death, "the freest, brotherliest, bravest human soul mine ever came in contact with. I call him on the whole the best man I have ever, after trial enough, found in this world or now hope to find." [21]

In July of 1831, Irving mentioned in a letter to a friend, "Two of my flock have received the gift of tongues and prophecy." [22] Two years earlier, in his "Homilies on Baptism," Irving had taken the established position of the Church of Scotland at that time, that the supernatural gifts of the Spirit had disappeared in the Church, and that one must distinguish between the outwardly manifested gifts of power and the inwardly manifested gift of sanctification. [23]

As firm and highly reflected as were his theological views, his sensitivity as a pastor would not allow him to remain shackled to a stated theological position where the spiritual care of one of his members was at stake. He counseled extensively with the individuals involved, and slowly satisfied himself that these were indeed genuine manifestations of the Holy Spirit.[24] Having come to this conclusion, with the single-minded sincerity which was his characteristic, Irving spoke out in favor of the movement, lending it the not inconsiderable weight of his reputation and pastoral office. In this regard it is worth noting that Irving himself never spoke in tongues, or interpreted, or prophesied[25] —at least not in the somewhat technical sense in which these terms were used within the movement—though his prayers for healing were not without effect.[26] But there is some evidence that he had the gift of discerning of spirits in no small measure, even if he did not so name it; the spiritual insight and authority with which he handled certain difficult situations points to more than ordinary pastoral perspicacity.[27]

Thus it was no light-headed enthusiasm which led Irving into the movement, but a sober theological reflection and pastoral concern, based on the opportunity to test the spiritual validity of these manifestations at first hand.

Though he did not at first permit it, Irving felt constrained at last to allow the utterance of tongues and prophecy in the regular worship service. The Trustees of the congregation took exception to this, and on communion Sunday, May 6, 1832, Irving found himself locked out of his church.[28] The Trustees refused to deal with the substantive issue of the manifestations themselves—whether they were genuine or not—but moved against Irving on the purely technical grounds that he had allowed persons not ordained by the Church of Scotland to 'minister' (speak in tongues and prophesy) in the church building.[29] (Not unlike several situations which have developed in the charismatic movement, where church authorities have sidestepped the issue of the charismata and dealt with a congregation or with a pastor simply on the basis of a mortgage or financial obligation which was owed a higher church authority.[30]) The greater part of Irving's congregation followed him. Before long, they had located a large picture gallery on Newman Street, and remodeled it into a meeting place for their church, which then continued to be one of the focal points of the movement.

The sight of the great man fallen from favor seemed to stir up the latent envy and vindictiveness which is never far from the scene where the small-minded encounter the great; his home presbytery in Scotland moved successfully to defrock Irving over a hair-splitting theological issue unrelated to the question of the charismata, a judgment acknowledged by every subsequent evaluation to have been an unconscionable blunder and miscarriage of justice. This humiliation, together with the ouster from his church, Irving bore with quiet dignity, and never a word of recrimination crossed his lips.

Irving lived scarcely more than two years from the founding of the church in Newman Street. In december of 1834, during a trip to Scotland in a weakened state of health, he succumbed to pneumonia and died, at the age of 42. Already, however, the leadership of the movement had passed to other hands. After the initial spread of the movement, Irving, despite his fame and his not inconsiderable gifts, was destined to play a less prominent role. While others were called to higher offices in the emerging order of the Catholic Apostolic Church, Irving was called simply to be the chief pastor, or bishop, of the one congregation in Newman Street. In nothing is the stature of the man more to be seen than in the quiet humility with which he accepts this minor role. In later years, some of his biographers would inveigh against the rank ingratitude of those who offered him no higher place, when he had risked everything for them.[31] But the remonstrance carries little real weight, for it can summon up no shred of support from the man himself.

Irving saw the whole thing from a different perspective. As he continued to weigh the development of the work, he came to the settled conviction—strongly reiterated in two letters to his congregation just a few weeks before his death [32]—that the emerging order of the Catholic Apostolic Church, like the initial manifestations of spiritual gifts, was a genuine work of the Holy Spirit. "Granting this miraculous postulate," his chief biographer wrote, "there is, in everything Irving does thereafter, a certain lofty reasonableness." [33]

"He could have run rough-shod over us all," recalled Henry Drummond, one of the leaders of the movement. But he accepted a subordinate position without a murmur and rendered spiritual obedience to those who were his own children in the faith.[34]

Irving's contemporaries outside the Catholic Apostolic Church thought him deluded. Some 30 years after his death, Carlyle said to a visiting American: "My poor friend Irving! Men thought him *daft:* but he was *dazed.* I have heard it said that the eagle becomes blind in gazing with unveiled eyes upon the sun. Thus Irving tried to do what no man may do and live— to gaze full into the brightness of Deity, and so blindness fell upon him." [35] A recent student of Irving's life, however, states that "it is impossible to dismiss him as one who was unbalanced or deluded. All his writings during his last years reveal a lucid and ordered mind, unfolding a complete theological system. Even his last letter, dated Glasgow, 21st November, 1834, and addressed to his father-in-law, shows a clear and unimpaired mind." [36]

A sober reading of the evidence, in the light of the Church's experience with the Pentecostal, and more recently with the charismatic movement, renders possible a new understanding of Irving's place in Church history: He was a man ahead of his time, pointing to things yet future for the great body of the Church. He was a forerunner not only of the Catholic Apostolic Church in a direct sense, but of the entire Pentecostal phenomenon of the 20th century. The things he said and did, his emphases and concerns, largely rejected in his own day, have become commonplace in the Pentecostal and neo-Pentecostal movements of our time.

Two years before the revival of spiritual gifts, Irving had spoken of himself with a certain prophetic presentiment, in the dedication to a volume of sermons: "I am but a rough, rude man, like my fathers, formed for border warfare, as God may please to call me; to hew wood and draw water for the camp of the saints. Yet will I fight for the king with the spiritual weapons of our warfare until the end; though I be rather a sort of pioneer and forerunner. . . ." [37] It was altogether fitting, and not a little ironic, that when he was buried in the Glasgow Cathedral, the window above Edward Irving's crypt should be a portrayal of John the Baptist.

CHAPTER FIVE

The Church: The Body of Christ

Near the outbreak of the movement, certain words of prophecy were spoken which had little apparent meaning for the immediate hearers, but which portended a significant development in the future of the Catholic Apostolic Church. In 1830, at a prayer meeting in the MacDonald household in Port Glasgow, the word was spoken, "Send us *apostles*, send *apostles, apostles*, to prepare the Bride!" [38] In Bavaria, two years earlier, in a Roman Catholic cottage meeting, came the word: "Thus saith the Lord, I will again send you *apostles* and *prophets*, as at the beginning, and I will pour out my Spirit as in former times." [39] The promise that God would restore the ancient ordinances of the Church continued to be voiced in words of prophecy, though it seems that no clear idea of what this meant or would involve was prevalent in the movement.

On October 31, 1832, at a prayer meeting in Irving's home, Henry Drummond, a wealthy businessman and sometime member of Parliament, who was deeply committed to the movement, approached John Bate Cardale, a prominent London lawyer who was kneeling, and had just finished praying for the Church, that she might be clothed with power from on high. Drummond spoke with what was later remembered as 'indescribable power and dignity,' naming Cardale to the office of apostle.[40] A week later, on November 7, the call was repeated, this time through Edward Taplin, later to be named the chief prophet of the movement.[41] Thus emerged into view that which was to become the signal characteristic and claim of the Catholic Apostolic Church, the restoration of the charismatic offices in the Church.

Over the next two years, eleven other men were called, by prophetic utterance, to complete the college of apostles. Men were called to numerous other offices as well: prophets, evangelists, pastors and teachers; 'Angels' (their term for local bishop, or chief pastor of a congregation), elders, deacons; and miscellaneous assisting ministries. On July 14, 1835, the twelve apostles were formally set apart for their calling. Thus, within the relatively short

42

space of five years, a spontaneous movement of considerable diversity had crystallized into one of the most highly formalized ecclesiastical structures in all of Church history. Yet the spontaneity and flexibility of the movement, its sense of purpose and mission, its spiritual sensitivity and quest, and the involvement of its members in a variety of experiences and tasks, was maintained and developed in remarkable degree, as the history of the next several decades amply demonstrates.

The first action the apostles was to remain quiet for twelve months, an accomplishment so uncharacteristic of ecclesiastical officials in general, and of newly appointed clerics in particular, that it must be remarked as one of the more compelling evidences of divine inspiration . . .

Together with seven of the prophets, they lived in seclusion at Albury, where daily they prayed and studied through the Bible together. Their study and concern came to center upon the nature and destiny of the Church. Through prophetic revelation, the Mosaic Tabernacle was set forth as a type of the Christian Church, in considerable detail.[42] The history, worship, order, ministry, and present condition of the Church were considered with great thoroughness.

43

The great bulk of Catholic Apostolic literature has to do with the nature and structure of the Church. It was more than a myopic preoccupation with proper form and order. Even where one might judge that it was carried to extremes, it was nevertheless rooted in the conviction that the Church has a certain God-given constitution; only as the eternal ordinances of God are put into effect, can the Church become that spiritual dwelling place of God in which He makes Himself known.[43]

This is a far cry from the free-wheeling ecclesiology with which most Protestants are familiar—where church structures are more likely to pattern themselves after the successful American corporation, or a state legislature, than any supposed pattern to be found in Scripture. Even Roman Catholic thinking on the structure of the Church seems to find itself less and less comfortable with a 'revealed ecclesiology.' A recent Catholic study of the ministry comes to the conclusion that tradition and theology "reveal the radically historical nature of the church which reacts *in a most human manner* to the inevitable impact of cultural change in its constant effort to serve the gospel. The tradition of fidelity and creativity liberates us from the forms of the past while inspiring us with the

44

courage to grow in service. Theology stimulates us *to consider alternative models of office* in faithful continuity with our past and open to the needs of the present and the future [italics ours]." [44]

The Catholic Apostolic Church understanding of the Church proceeds along quite different lines: What is the Church? It is the Body of Christ, a body in which all members share the same life. This unity of life constitutes the Church an *organism*. St. Paul emphasizes the organic structure of the Church when he speaks of it as the Body of Christ. "As the body of a man was so fashioned by God that its life should find full expression through its several organs, so was it with the body of Christ; through its several ministries this new and supernatural life is to find its full expression. If man can add no new organ to his own body, much less can he add a new ministry to the Church. Nor can he enlarge or diminish the function of any. He can, indeed, refuse to use the means by which his own bodily life is nourished and strengthened, and so bring in a state of weakness in which all the organs shall be unable to perform their full functions; and he can mutilate his body by the destruction of an organ, but the organic structure remains. The eye-ball may per-

45

ish, the empty socket remains to tell where it has been, and where, if vision is restored, it must be set again. In like manner the life of the body of Christ—the Church—may be weakened through the unbelief and disobedience of its members, grieving the Holy Ghost, and separating it from its Head, and its ministries be unable fully to perform their functions, and some apparently be lost; but the Church remains the same organic structure which God constituted it to be. The Holy Ghost may be unable, for a time, to use all its ministries as the instruments of His operation, but they abide as structural parts, ready to be used by Him when He can again put forth the fulness of His power." [45]

The chief corollary which proceeds from this understanding of the Church as in truth a body is the conviction that the primary organ in the body—that upon which its unity and health depends—is the *Apostleship*. No understanding of the history, life, and teachings of the Catholic Apostolic Church is possible until one grasps this central thesis. It is absolutely determinative of their doctrine of the Church, and their understanding of Church history. "Apostles, and apostles alone, are in Scripture declared to be the centre of authority, of doctrine, of unity, in all things, to the

46

visible Church of Christ on earth, until His second and glorious appearing to those that look for Him, without sin unto salvation. And accordingly, in the history of the Church in the Acts of the Apostles, it is declared that the converts at the first continued steadfastly in the *apostles'* doctrine and fellowship. . . . Apostles are the foundations of the Church; not of this Church, or of the other, but of the One, Holy, Catholic Church, hence Apostolic; they are the base whereon the lively stones should be builded, and the perpetual means of sustaining and upholding the fabric of the Living Temple, the Church, in unity of spirit and life of doctrine and of government." [46]

The uniqueness of the Apostolic office is that it is appointed directly by Christ.[47] Not even apostles can appoint other apostles; the idea of 'apostolic succession' is contrary to the essential constitution of the Church.[48] "Apostles could bring bishops into their place, as heads of the several churches. More than this they could not do."[49]

How, then, has this office continued in the Church, if not by some kind of succession? The answer of the Catholic Apostolic Church is that the office did *not* continue. "While the memory of the Apostles has been loaded with honours all but divine, they were in their own lifetime many times despised and set at nought, both by churches and individuals; and God suffered the will of man to prevail, and withdrew the authority which was resisted, and the holy rule and discipline which the unholy could not endure." [50] The Church refused to press on to perfection, as the Apostle Paul had urged them. "The punishment was the postponement of the Lord's return, and the loss of the Apostolic office. It was with her as with Israel of old. After the giving of the law at Mt. Sinai (which answered to the Christian Pentecost), a few months would have sufficed to take the tribes into the promised land, and their forty years of wandering in the wilderness were the fruit and chastisement of their unbelief. . . . This failure of the Church finds analogy in all the preceding dispensations. God has always suffered Himself to be defeated at the first, that the weakness and instability of the creature might be fully manifested, and the glory of the final victory be given to Him alone." [51]

This gives us the key to the Catholic Apostolic Church's reading of Church history: Not the story of a mighty Church, moving toward perfection in the power of the Risen Christ, but a weakened and crippled Church, still living by the grace of God through the ministries which remain, but lacking that one foundational ministry without which she can never reach perfection. Their detailed, and by no means superficial, analysis of the history of the Church proceeds from this basic assumption. Their doctrine of the Church, and prescription for renewal, likewise revolves around their understanding of the Apostleship as the chief ordinance given by Christ for the building of His Church.

The claim of the Catholic Apostolic Church was that in their Work, God had restored this foundational ministry to His Church.[52] Their chief historian says that this is the basic question which the various branches of Christendom must face, in regard to their Work: "Has the living God revealed Himself here as He did at the beginning? Has He truly called and sent forth Apostles?"[53]

Dr. P. E. Shaw, in his history of the Catholic Apostolic Church, handles the question in this way: "Though not accepted as Apostles, they may yet be recognized as 'apostolic' men. Moreover they are not in the regular course of ministerial appointments, but have been rather men sent from God, starting a new line of succession. . . . God may start in the course of history a new departure and has often done so . . . men sent from God in this way would include Peter Waldo, Martin Luther, John Calvin, John Wesley. . . ." [54] Kilian McDonnell, a Roman Catholic scholar, in considering the ways of validating Christian ministry, concludes that "what is essential is apostolic life, faith, service, and authority . . . which can take various ministerial forms." [55] Measured by such criteria, the Catholic Apostolic Church may indeed be enrolled in the company of those who have ministered the grace vouchsafed to them by God. Whatever more they may have been, or may yet be, in the purposes of God, must be left open to the judgment of history.

The Catholic Apostolic Church's generally fair and balanced evaluation of the various historical streams in Christendom remains remarkably free of the sectarian spirit which one has come to expect from exclusivistic revival movements. An Anglo-Catholic clergyman, who made a life-long study of the Catholic Apostolic Church, and was advisor to the Archbishop of Canterbury on the subject, stated, "There was no breakaway from the Historic Church [by the Catholic Apostolic Church]. It was not and is not Dissent at all, because before you can dissent you must have first assented, before you can break away you

50

must have first been joined. *It was a Movement from without the Historic Church towards it* ... [italics ours]. By its century of witness to many under-valued or forgotten truths ... its beauty of worship ... and its power of forming Christian character of primitive but Catholic type ... it reveals the abiding of the Holy Spirit. Too great a charity towards other churches, even in times of intolerance, has informed the Catholic Apostolics for any intolerance on the part of the Church to be justified." [56]

The issue of this year in retreat, and proof of the maturing ecumenical vision which was developing in the Catholic Apostolic Church, was the sending out of the twelve apostles to the various countries of Christendom. They carried with them their "Testimony Addressed to the Rulers in Church and State in Christian Lands," one of the most remarkable documents in the literature of the Catholic Apostolic Church.[57] In this document the evils pervading society are traced to their spiritual source, in the Church's departure from God's essential ordinances (both in Church and in state); and God's means for restoring the same are set forth. They were to seek contact with Pope, with bishops, with kings, presenting their testimony

51

wherever it would be received. Yet the greater burden of their commission was to "mine for gold," i.e., to go out in the character of private individuals, as learners and observers, rather than as teachers; to discover in the various countries of Christendom those elements of worship, church order, and spiritual life which belonged to the Church Universal.[58]

Returning from their journeyings, the apostles gradually introduced into the life and worship of their congregations those elements which accorded with their vision of a restored Church. Worship took on a decidedly more 'Catholic' flavor, with the introduction of vestments, and an elaborate liturgy. The various kinds of ministry, both for the Church Universal and for local congregations, were more and more carefully set forth. The life and worship of the churches was set in order, as they believed, according to a divinely revealed pattern.

It was not the intention of the Catholic Apostolic Church to win large numbers to their movement, or to become another denomination in Christendom. From the beginning, and throughout their history, the prophecies had made clear that they were to be a 'model,'[59] a Church within the Church, demonstrating the principles and practices by which she might be restored to her true constitution and calling. Thus they saw their mission as directed primarily to the Church, rather than to the world.[60]

Yet they saw in "the Work" (as it was most often called within the Catholic Apostolic Church itself) more than an interesting display about which other Christians might speculate. They saw it as God's first step toward the 'restoration of all things,' which would culminate in the return of Christ.[61] Their mission and calling was to let God's divine pattern for His Church be worked out in them, as a 'first fruit.'[62] When and how God might use the Work was His own business. Thus their virtual disregard either for expanding or perpetuating themselves as a body.

Yet a Church claiming such a mission, and such a body of revelation, could not help but attract followers. During the next decade it spread out and founded new congregations, principally in England, Scotland, Germany, Canada, and the United States. The apostles and prophets continued to order the life of the congregations according to their understanding of the revelation. And not without effect. For however one may judge the authenticity or validity of their revelations, the high level of worship, dedicated leadership, spiritual instruction, pastoral care, practical service, and personal piety which was fostered in the Catholic Apostolic Church cannot be gainsaid.[63]

The history of the Catholic Apostolic Church in the ensuing decades is primarily a history of the development of its faith and life along the lines of its essential understanding and insight.

CHAPTER SIX

The Baptism with the Holy Spirit

In the Catholic Apostolic Church, an exclusive focus upon the spiritual gifts moderated considerably as the movement matured. Yet the central insight, that the life and power of the Church utterly depends upon the Holy Spirit, remained a cornerstone of their faith.

In 1847, John Cardale, 'the pillar of the apostles,' shared with his fellow apostles a "crisis of apathy" which had been reported to him by a number of the bishops. A feeling of deadness, a lack of conscious spiritual life and power seemed to pervade the churches. The apostles' answer to this crisis was to institute the "rite of sealing," whereby the Holy Spirit should be conveyed to the baptized in special measure, through the laying on of the apostles' hands. For, "assuming that the churches were instructed and built upon the foundations, the mode of going on to perfection was clearly the giving of the Holy Ghost by an outward act of laying on of hands." [64] This had been hinted at in prophecy twelve years earlier, but only now did they grasp its significance.[65] Thus, faced with a dwindling of spiritual life, the apostles recalled their people to the initial revelation, that *power for the Church is to be sought nowhere else than in a fresh outpouring of the Holy Spirit.*

This crisis crystallized the theology of the Catholic Apostolic Church concerning the baptism with the Holy Spirit. As early as 1832, Irving had seen these happenings in relation to Christian baptism: "No one doubteth that Christian baptism doth convey to the believer the gift of repentance towards God, and the remission of sins by the regeneration of the Holy Spirit; and why should they doubt that it doth convey also the baptism with the Holy Ghost for speaking in tongues and prophesyings?" [66] John Cardale, in his two-volume work, *Readings Upon the Liturgy*, which, despite its unpretentious title, is the definitive theological work of the Catholic Apostolic Church, elaborates the view that two distinct operations of the Holy Spirit are involved: "There is a gift of the Holy Ghost which Christ sends down and imparts after Baptism, and to those already baptized . . .

to be distinguished from baptism with water." [67]

In treating the biblical material, Cardale uses the terms "receiving the Holy Spirit," "baptism with the Holy Spirit," "the gift of the Holy Spirit" more-or-less interchangeably,[68] following the pattern of Acts, where Peter successively uses each of these to describe the self-same event (see Acts 10:47, 11:16, 11:17). The term, however, which became formalized in the order of the Catholic Apostolic Church was "sealing with the Holy Spirit."

The effect or purpose of this rite was to equip the believer for service in the Body of Christ: "To the reception of the promised Gift of the Holy Ghost, every baptized man is bound to press forward. He that is baptized into Christ, and is not filled with the Spirit of Christ dwelling in him, so that he may be ready at all times to speak the words and do the works of God, according to God's good pleasure and his place in the Body of Christ—that man fails of the grace in which every baptized man should stand. And when this failure is not confined to individuals, but extends to the whole community . . . it is impossible that God's people should continue to realize their calling . . . we insist, therefore, on the necessity of the Rite of Sealing. . . ." [69]

How was this "sealing" to be received? In one way only: Through the laying on of the apostles' hands. "The giving of the Holy Ghost by the laying on of the apostles' hands . . . is the means appointed of God whereby the baptized members of the Body of Christ are made partakers of the Holy Ghost. The form of expression used is 'Receive the Holy Ghost.' " [70]

Thus, what had begun as a spontaneous outpouring of the Spirit, with charismatic manifestations, became structured into the formal order and liturgy of the Catholic Apostolic Church as the Rite of Sealing. Along with the sealing, which they saw as God's means of equipping a believer for service in the Body of Christ, came a distinct soft-pedaling of the charismatic manifestations. In preparing the people to receive this rite, the apostles "sought to disabuse them of the idea that because, at the beginning, the laying on of hands was, in most cases, followed by tongues and prophesying, therefore that some outward manifestation, or inward consciousness of spiritual grace or power was to be expected or looked for, as proof of the reality of the gift conferred. . . . Hardly an instance occurred of any individual commencing to speak with tongues or prophesy at the time of receiving the laying on of hands. Should such a case occur, it would be necessary to stop it, as being an interruption of the service." [71]

The exegetical basis for this development raises some questions. Cardale says, "There is no example in Scripture of the Gift of the Holy Ghost being bestowed through any other *ordinance*, but only by the imposition of the hands of the apostles." [72] He cites Acts 8:14-17, in which the Gift of the Holy Spirit was indeed given through the laying on of the apostles' hands. It may be argued, however, whether this was the necessary, or even normal, experience in the primitive Christian community. The outpouring on the Day of Pentecost was the spontaneous and sovereign action of Christ himself, as was the outpouring in the household of Cornelius (Acts 10); Paul appears to have received the Holy Spirit through the ministry of Ananias (Acts 9:17-18). And in writing to the Galatians, Paul suggests that they received the Spirit by "hearing with faith" (Gal. 3:2). The matter is further complicated when it is maintained that the Gift of the Holy Spirit was meant only for those who were at least twenty years of age, and who had attained to a degree of spiritual maturity. [73] It seems quite clear in Acts, that the baptism with the Holy Spirit functions as an aspect

59

of initiation into the life of the Christian community; [74] in every case where it occurs after Pentecost, it is with new converts.

Nevertheless, the rite of sealing was not without a considerable effect in the life of the Catholic Apostolic Church. "The mere announcement of the purpose of the apostles to give the laying on of hands produced its immediate effect in reviving the spirits of the people . . . and the fruit of the endowment with the Holy Spirit of God in those to whom the rite of sealing had been administered was not long in showing itself." [75] The immediate 'fruit' of this experience was not an increase in charismatic manifestations, which had been somewhat discouraged, but a deepened concern for developing the *worship* of the Church. The congregations appealed to the apostles for further instruction. Out of this developed their rich liturgical tradition, which one Anglican cleric says "pales the richest revision of the Book of Common Prayer into insignificance." [76] It becomes clear, as one studies the literature of the Catholic Apostolic Church, that the rite of sealing formed a watershed in their experience and development. It was like a new Pentecost, which continued as long as the apostles remained alive.

In the present-day charismatic movement, also, people speak about "the baptism with the Holy Spirit." One will not be in touch with the charismatic movement very long before he hears this term, often framed in a direct, personal question: "Have you received the baptism with the Holy Spirit?"

Some of this is due to a direct borrowing from classical Pentecostalism, where it forms a basic component of their experience and theology. Yet there has also been a good deal of first-hand reflection upon the biblical material, in the light of experience within the charismatic movement itself. The fact that this theological category was considered with some thoroughness in the Catholic Apostolic Church, which in turn recognized certain roots of this in the Church Fathers,[77] seems to indicate that in any case we are dealing here with a basic biblical category, and not a recent sectarian aberration.

In the charismatic movement, pastors and theologians have dealt with the question of the baptism with the Holy Spirit in a variety of ways. J. Rodman Williams, a Presbyterian professor of systematic theology, says, "In receiving baptism long ago, I was not only baptized in water but also *in the Holy Spirit*. I have been led within the past few years into such an *appropriation* of my early baptism in the Holy Spirit that it was actually *a receiving* of this baptism. . . . It was 'joy unspeakable,' reality amazing, upsurge of 'heavenly language'— glory! I *received* my baptism in the Holy Spirit." [78]

This is somewhat reminiscent of Edward Irving, who saw the baptism with the Holy Spirit linked more-or-less organically to baptism in water. Classical Pentecostalism speaks in terms of a 'second experience,' subsequent to salvation. The focus of the salvation experience is upon 'new birth,' receiving the new life in Christ; the focus of the baptism with the Holy Spirit is upon power for ministry, with the initial sign of speaking in tongues. Neither experience is dependent upon baptism, as such, though baptism is a normal part of Pentecostal initiation. The Catholic Apostolic Church, as we have seen, saw baptism as conveying spiritual *life*, and the baptism with the Holy Spirit ('sealing') as conveying *ability to minister* in the Body of Christ, with no immediate charismatic manifestation, but a definite expectation of 'fruit.'

David du Plessis, a classical Pentecostal who has had wide influence in the charismatic movement, reminds us that we encounter Jesus in a variety of roles—Savior,

Lord, Healer, etc.—and challenges us to encounter Him also as the Baptizer with the Holy Spirit. This emphasis, of course, tends to focus upon an encounter with Christ, rather than a stereotyped 'experience,' and opens the door to a wider variety of responses.

Arnold Bittlinger, a German pastor and theologian, speaks of a release of the Spirit, in which the potential which one receives upon becoming a Christian may be actualized in a variety of ways, including charismatic manifestations.[79] This emphasis sets charismatic manifestations into a broad spectrum of experiences which a Christian may have: conversion, spiritual gifts, union with Christ, etc.

Joseph Hogan, a Roman Catholic bishop, sees the baptism with the Holy Spirit as a flowering or actualization of baptismal grace,[80] a view similar to that of Williams and Bittlinger, and especially meaningful for churches with a sacramental tradition.

It is evident that no clear-cut theological formulation of this phenomenon has yet emerged in the charismatic movement. What we have at present is a variety of ways for describing and explaining what is the same essential reality or experience.

The experience of the Catholic Apostolic Church may indicate that variety at this

63

point could be a healthy thing for the Church. When they formalized their theology and practice in regard to the baptism with the Holy Spirit, as we have seen, their exegesis of the biblical passages, and their subsequent practice, became somewhat forced and wooden; and there was a definite diminishing of charismatic manifestations.

The biblical passages dealing with the baptism with the Holy Spirit, especially in Acts, almost defy any attempts at systematization. And the kinds of experience which people are having in the charismatic movement also resist our efforts to cram them into a neat pre-conceived pattern. "The Spirit blows where it wills" (John 3:8). Our theological description of His presence and activity in the Church must remain sufficiently flexible to take into account His oftentimes exasperating inconsistencies!

The point on which there seems to be wide agreement within the charismatic movement is the fact that God *does* give something to Christians in the way of a definite experience of the Holy Spirit's power and gifts. Whether one believes that this is given *in* one's Christian initiation (the 'organic' view), or *because* one is a Christian (the classical Pentecostal view) is a question for further theological study. It may be that a variety of formulations, like the paradoxical theorems of modern physics, comes closest to expressing the whole truth.

One aspect of the question, however, which has received too little attention is its application to the Church, as a *Body*. The discussions have focused almost exclusively on the individual, and his personal experience of the baptism with the Holy Spirit. The Catholic Apostolic Church saw the question relating primarily to the Church, and only secondarily to the individual.

We can speak with far greater definiteness about the effect of the baptism with the Holy Spirit upon a congregation as a whole than upon any particular individual within that congregation. It is something like the actuarial tables of an insurance company: They can predict the health and longevity patterns of a group of people with a high degree of accuracy, but cannot apply those findings rigidly to any given individual within the group. It is important to ask what the baptism with the Holy Spirit means for the individual Christian. But equally important to ask what effect it is likely to have in a congregation.

We have lived with this experience in our congregation since 1961, and we have been privileged to have wide contacts with other individuals, groups, and congregations who have had extensive, and, in some cases, long-termed charismatic experiences. Several things come into focus when we see the baptism with the Holy Spirit in its *corporate* dimension, over an extended period of time—

(1) *We can vary the terminology.* Peter used four different terms to describe the self-same event, the outpouring of the Holy Spirit in the household of Cornelius: "These people have *received the Holy Spirit* just as we have.... As I began to speak, *the Holy Spirit fell on* them just as on us at the beginning. And I remembered the word of the Lord, 'You shall be *baptized with the Holy Spirit.'* ... God gave the same *gift* to them ..." (Acts 10:47, 11:15-17). One person in a congregation may speak of "receiving the baptism" (with the Holy Spirit), while another describes it as a "release of the Spirit," or another as "the gift of the Spirit." In some denominations or religious traditions, one expression may prove appropriate, while others raise unnecessary objections and could just as easily be abandoned. The Scripture offers us sufficient variety so that we need not make mere terminology a matter of offense or misunderstanding.

(2) *We should expect definite results.*

66

On the one hand, it is true that the moment we stereotype the results of the baptism with the Holy Spirit for an *individual*, we begin to exclude some people from meaningful participation in it. The Holy Spirit deals with each person in His own sovereign way. But, on the other hand, what we cannot do in terms of the individual, we can and must do in regard to the congregation as a whole. When we present Jesus as the Baptizer with the Holy Spirit, we should expect a wide variety of concrete results in the congregation. The gifts and the fruit of the Holy Spirit should come into noticeable manifestation.

When a congregation ceases to expect and experience results, it is a sign that the baptism with the Holy Spirit has been relegated to the category of mere doctrine —a truth that may be believed in a theoretical sense, but which has no more concrete effect on a congregation's life than belief that the moon is made of volcanic rock.

When the Catholic Apostolic Church began to circumscribe their expectations of what the Holy Spirit might do, as we have seen, there was a distinct fall-off in charismatic experience. A too-great concern for order and liturgical correctness, so far as we can determine, appears to have had the effect of unnecessarily quenching the

Spirit. It may be that Dr. Shaw's judgment is too extreme: "The freedom and frequency of supernatural utterance was checked and suppressed until it became almost extinct." [81] Rossteuscher, the chief historian of the movement, suggests rather that the gifts continued to be manifested, but in a more regularized way.[82] It is evident that very real fruit was experienced, as the rite of sealing was practiced in their churches. But one questions whether that could not have been just as fully experienced, without artificially curtailing the charismatic power and expression, to the probable detriment of the Church.

It is a great first step when a congregation comes to accept the *doctrine* that Jesus baptizes with the Holy Spirit. But that belief must lead, *and continue to lead*, into the experience of the Holy Spirit's power!

Paradoxically, concrete results in the congregation are most certain to come about when we prescribe little in the way of specific expectations in regard to individual members. If we tell people that the baptism with the Holy Spirit will give them joy, or boldness for witnessing, or the gift of prophecy, or tongues, then that is what they will be programmed to expect. But what if the Holy Spirit has another plan, another gift, for this person at this time? Some people come into a new dimension of spiritual life quickly, even dramatically, through the baptism with the Holy Spirit; for others, it is a gradual unfolding. If we allow for and expect this kind of variety, the Holy Spirit will bring forth no lack of concrete results in the congregation as a whole.

(3) *The gifts of the Holy Spirit, including speaking in tongues, are a normal part of the experience.* Recall, again, that this is said with regard to the congregation as a whole, not an individual, as such. It is not possible, on the basis of Scripture or of experience, to say that every individual who experiences the baptism with the Holy Spirit will speak in tongues. But neither can we find scriptural support to say that *none* will speak in tongues. In a congregation where Christ is presented not only as the Lamb of God who takes away the sin of the world, but also as the Baptizer with the Holy Spirit, we should expect that speaking in tongues will be experienced in that congregation.

We mention speaking in tongues in particular because this is the gift around which most of the controversy and misunderstanding rages. Opponents of tongues object

69

quite rightly when this gift is over-empha-
sized, or when brash and silly opinions are
voiced concerning it. ("You don't have the
Holy Spirit unless you've spoken in
tongues.") We do not hold or support such
views. But we *do* believe that "God has
appointed *in the Church* . . . speakers in
tongues" (1 Cor. 12:28). If there are *none*
who speak in tongues, the Church is lacking a gift which God considered important
for her life and ministry.

We have never counted noses in our congregation to find out who speaks in tongues
and who does not. I know many who have
received this gift, and there are undoubted-
ly some who have experienced it privately,
and have not bothered to tell me about
it. It is not emphasized all that much. (In
the early stages of charismatic renewal
in a given fellowship, speaking in tongues
quite naturally comes in for a good bit
of attention; as the movement develops and
matures, tongues settles more into a position of 'quiet availability.')

It is true that speaking in tongues was
experienced widely in apostolic times, and
that it has had a special significance in
the spread of the Pentecostal and charismatic movements. It may well be that it
does have a special relationship to the baptism with the Holy Spirit. But we must

70

also recognize the fact that even in Pentecostal churches not everyone speaks in tongues, and that there is no clear scriptural warrant to believe that they will. As a pastor, it does not disturb me that some of my members do not speak in tongues. I feel no urgency to highlight this particular gift, except as a member might inquire about it, or as it would come up in a sermon text or Bible study. Yet, if *nobody* in the congregation had this gift, then I would be concerned—just as I would be concerned if I discovered that nobody was praying, nobody was studying Scripture, nobody was being healed, nobody was giving, nobody was growing in holiness. These are the kind of things which *should* be happening in a normal congregation.

Much of the controversy over spiritual gifts would be ameliorated if we began to look at the congregation as a Body, rather than looking exclusively at individual members and their experience. The word must be proclaimed *to the Body*: "Earnestly desire the spiritual gifts!" (2 Cor. 14:1). The Spirit will apply that word as He wills, and we will see the various gifts coming into manifestation. Until and unless they do, there will be no renewal in the Church. Human improvisations cannot substitute for the gifts of the Holy Spirit which God has provided for His Church. When the Holy Spirit is released in the life of a congregation, there *will* be speakers in tongues, healers, teachers, helpers—the whole range of divinely appointed gifts and ministries. We should rest content with nothing less. "The Church," wrote the chief American clergyman of the Catholic Apostolic Church, "is a Divine workmanship as truly as the body of a man, which is its best and most adequate symbol; it requires a diversity of ministries and gifts to fulfill the purpose of God in its creation: these are set by Him, and are not of man's appointment, and *none of them can be lost without injury to the whole* [italics ours]." [83]

CHAPTER SEVEN

Unity in the Body of Christ

The single greatest criticism leveled against the charismatic movement is that it breeds divisiveness. The generally healthy and orderly expression of spiritual gifts in the Catholic Apostolic Church was largely due to the kind of leadership which was exercised by those in authority. On the one hand, they welcomed the gifts, recognizing their validity and value for the Church as a whole; yet, on the other hand, they did not abdicate their leadership responsibility, but provided pastoral oversight so that the gifts would be used, and would develop, in the most helpful way.

The pattern of leadership in today's charismatic movement is somewhat checkered. Protestant denominational officials have generally failed to exercise effective leadership. They have too much conveyed the attitude that the charismatic movement is a fad, a sideline, an aberration; "go over in your corner and play with your blocks if you want to, but make sure that you don't disturb any of the grown-ups. . . ." This pat-them-on-the-head-and-hope-they'll-be-mollified approach has caused no little amount of the dissension. And small wonder. For it belittles an experience of tremendous, even transforming, significance, for the person who has had it. When a person's religious experience is at best tolerated, or at worst outlawed, one can hardly expect to see healthy spiritual growth and development. Church officials must recognize their own measure of responsibility for some of the unwholesome developments of the charismatic movement, *for they have in too many cases abdicated responsible and caring leadership.*

When responsible leadership is not given, the door is opened to immature and irresponsible leadership. And then the very kinds of abuse and distortion which church officials feared come to pass. Not because people involved in the charismatic movement are more unruly or self-willed than other Christians, but because they, like the others, also need pastoral oversight and care.

Church leaders who try to sweep the charismatic movement under the rug with one hand, cannot in good conscience point with the other hand at the divisiveness which it seems to cause. For an attitude of official rejection (however subtly camouflaged) is a major ingredient of the dissension. By failing to exercise effective leadership, which could lead to a wholesome integration of the charismatic movement into the life of the Church, they have allowed their people to become 'disordered by default.'

The Roman Catholic Church in the United States has generally handled things more effectively than the Protestants in regard to the charismatic movement. We know of no single Roman Catholic cleric who has been forced to leave his parish because of the charismatic movement. The reason is to be found in the kind of official stance which the leaders of the Roman Catholic Church have taken. In 1969, the National Conference of Catholic Bishops issued a statement in which they evaluated the charismatic movement in a generally positive way. They concluded their statement with this paragraph:

"It is the conclusion to the Committee on Doctrine that the movement should at this point not be inhibited but allowed to develop. Certain cautions, however, must be expressed. Proper supervision can be effectively exercised only if the Bishops keep in mind their pastoral responsibility to oversee and guide this movement in the

Church. We must be on guard that they avoid the mistakes of classic Pentecostalism. It must be recognized that in our culture there is a tendency to substitute religious experience for religious doctrine. In practise *we recommend that Bishops involve prudent priests to be associated with this movement. Such involvement and guidance would be welcome by the Catholic Pentecostals.*" (Italics ours.)

This is the kind of leadership which offers the best possibility for incorporating the values of the charismatic movement into the Church, while at the same time curbing any wrong tendencies. The two major Presbyterian bodies in the United States have issued reports which are generally positive and helpful. It is to be hoped that other church bodies will follow this kind of example—not only in terms of official reports, but also in the unofficial attitudes which filter down to the parish level. The charismatic movement needs both the acceptance and the authority of the Church; we will have more to say on this in chapter nine. The point we make here is that the primary responsibility for maintaining unity rests with the leadership of the Church.

This, in turn, leads us to a consideration of how unity can be achieved among the leaders themselves. In illustrating this, we will focus upon leadership at the parish or group level, where we have had practical experience. The principles, however, could well have application at higher levels of church authority.

The Catholic Apostolic Church believed that the unity of the Church centered in the college of the Apostles. "The individual churches [in New Testament times] were not so many isolated and independent bodies which being brought into existence, were left to themselves, and whose preservation and growth depended solely on the ministries and gifts within themselves; but the common band which united all Churches, the divine ordinance by which many congregations constituted *one church* was the Apostleship. The Apostles and their fellow-labourers, through whose ministry the individual Churches were brought into existence, continued to be the living centre, from which, under the continual rule of Christ Himself, new blessings were always flowing. Through them all the Churches scattered over many lands were kept in unity of faith and of the Holy Ghost, preserved from errors and heresies, advanced in the fear of God, and in holy discipline, and ever anew enriched with spiritual blessings. Each Church was subject to the guides and rulers given to it of God, and these again were subject to the Lord *in His Apostles* [italics ours], were followers of them, as they were followers of Christ; thus was the whole body knit together by bands and ordinances given by God." [84]

The Catholic Apostolic Church applied this basic understanding to the men called to apostleship among them: "The apostles are the instrument through which the Lord Himself speaks from heaven, and carries out His work as the true Moses, the ultimate law-giver and ruler of the Church. Not as individuals, but only as a body, a unity, a college. When an apostle speaks or acts in virtue of his office, he always does so as representative of the Twelve, responsible to them. The Apostles 'build the heart of the Church', are the kernel of unity for all. The Church becomes one as she enters into the fellowship of the Apostles, receiving their teaching and order. Therefore the Apostles are warned above all else to maintain their unity. 'When one apostle says "No", you do not have the full mind of the Lord!' Only in matters of outward form did the apostles act by majority vote. *In all matters of substance they proceeded only by unanimous agreement* [italics ours]." [85]

The Episcopal Church of the Redeemer in Houston struck on something close to this during a renewal which began in the mid-1960's. From a nearly dead inner-city parish, they have been transformed into a vital Christian fellowship, with an outreach of ministry and social concern which has attracted national attention. Jerry Barker, one of their elders, visited in our congregation and shared with us some of the principles of renewal which they have discovered. One of the keys was something very much akin to the understanding of the Catholic Apostolic Church: a fellowship of elders. Jerry said: "Before a parish can be renewed, there must be at the center a group of men—pastor and elders—who share a common vision and who are totally committed to it and to each other. The renewal proceeds outward from the elders. Problems may come up, but they cannot break up the church, because of the strong core of unity which has been developed among the elders."

Though our two congregations had had no previous contact, we discovered that we shared a number of common insights, including this one. In the early 1960's, there was considerable controversy over the charismatic movement in our whole church body (the American Lutheran Church). When it came to a peak in our congregation, we discovered that there was a sharp division *within the Church Council*, which was telegraphed outward to the congregation. We passed through that stormy period, and entered into quieter waters. In 1965, Ernst Gleede, a Lutheran pastor from Germany, visited in our congregation during the Lenten season. He shared with us the practice which they had followed in a congregation he served in Germany, where they had experienced real awakening: "We never took action in the Church Council, on matters of substance, unless we were in unanimous agreement." The germ of this quite likely came through the writings of the Catholic Apostolic Church, for Pastor Gleede belongs to the Brethren of the Common Life, a Lutheran order with spiritual roots in the Catholic Apostolic Church.

In March of 1966, the man who was then president of our Church Council suggested this practice to our Council. It was never voted on; it was simply offered as a recommendation. But it took root. It has become the unwritten presupposition of everything we undertake. 'We move as one, or we move not at all.'

The effect has been nothing less than miraculous. There is spirited discussion, and strong opinions are voiced. But there is an almost total absence of defensiveness, because there is nothing to defend; every man knows that his vote, alone, can halt any action. It breeds a high level of responsibleness: On important matters, involving the faith and life of other people, it is awesome to know that one's voice carries that kind of weight. We have seen issues come to a point where all but one person were in agreement. The issue is tabled. The matter is prayed over, until the next meeting. (How the Holy Spirit thrives on patience, while the devil starves out!) Met again, we have seen the entire Council come around to the point-of-view of the one man who could not agree. Or, the one man now finds himself able to agree. Or, a new development enters the picture, and the Council finds a different point on which to hinge its agreement.

Agreement like this does not come easily or mechanically. It requires a radical openness on the part of the Council members. Openness to God, first of all. Without persistent prayer, it won't work. When we reach an impasse, or seem to have exhausted a topic without reaching agreement, one of the men will usually suggest that we stop and pray. Not for a minute or two, merely, but for ten or fifteen minutes; we once prayed for half an hour, and experienced such a sense of God's presence (with prophetic revelation), that we could do little more than smile and shake our heads when we met each other in the next several days.

Secondly, there must be an openness *to each other*. To move in unity does not mean that we reach total subjective agreement on every issue. Part of spiritual maturity is to recognize one's own areas of strength and weakness. One man, for instance, may have a keen sense of what is needed in the teaching ministry of the church. But when it comes to financial matters, he has neither faith nor vision. He comes to recognize in one or two of the others a vision in financial matters; this recognition is part of his integration into the unity of the Council. He may have opinions in financial matters, but he recognizes that these other men have a vision and an openness to the Spirit in that area which he lacks. And so he learns that there are times when the Spirit will allow him to *defer to his brethren,* even though he may still have questions and objections. He recognizes that in those instances, the Spirit wills to manifest His unity *through that brother.* Just as, at another time, when something concerning the teaching ministry of the Church is being considered, the Spirit may manifest unity through him. Yet none of this is so rigid that the Spirit cannot speak His mind through any member of the Council in a quite unexpected, yet clearly authentic, manner. Thus the unity of the Spirit is not a rubber-stamp, conformist unity, but a unity of *love*, a unity of *mutual regard*, a unity *in the Lord*.

Thirdly, there must be an openness *to the whole fellowship*. The ear of each Council member must be 'easily entreated.' Any member of the congregation, down to the least, should have access to the Council through one or more of the Council members—and not least their own wives. Some of the most necessary words—words of real prophetic significance—will come into the Council from the members. This highlights the essentially *servant* role of the Council. They are to take the various suggestions and concerns, and bring them before the Lord, on behalf of the congregation as a whole.

The result? Unity. Not superficial or forced, but substantial, deep. Men who are one because they have arrived at a specific point of agreement in the Lord. When this continues, over a period of months and years, something begins to happen in a congregation. The congregation begins to feel this unity. More than that, it is somehow *communicated* to them, not as 'information,' but as a living truth, a way of life. Which leads us to the statement of a basic principle: *That which the Lord gives to the Council, they can in turn give to the congregation.* The secret of unity in a congregation is to allow God first of all to work this unity in the Council.

This does not mean that a congregation will be without problems or complaints. But it creates in the Church Council a center of unity which can deal helpfully with issues that might otherwise divide a congregation. It takes into account the fact that 'babes in Christ' are not equipped for the same kind of ministry to which leaders are called. The babes are not always able to handle strong disagreements 'in the Spirit'; to make them party to it is as unwise as to visit upon young children the strong disagreements which their father and mother must work through from time to time. I am quite sure that some of the discussions which go on in the Church Council, were they thrown out into the congregation at large, would breed dissension, rivalry, discord. The insight of the Catholic Apostolic Church proves remarkably workable at the parish level: A congregation will experience unity as it enters into the unity which the Lord first works in the Church Council.

Another factor which we have become aware of only slowly, but which we now feel quite certain to be the case is this:

Those who are called to positions of leadership in a congregation or a fellowship become special candidates, as it were, for satanic assault; this often extends to their families as well. This is not to engender fear, but simply to alert one to the fact that we are engaged, as St. Paul tells us, in spiritual warfare.

Among the Council members we have come to recognize that what might pass as a rather normal discussion or decision in a secular setting, can be fraught with almost uncanny tensions and pressures in the setting of the church. At first we tended to dismiss this as some kind of orneriness peculiar to church members. But that is altogether too simplistic an answer, when one lives with people over an extended period of time, in a variety of situations. The more reasonable explanation is that Satan indeed would like to intensify his agitating activities where it would do the most good— for him. He knows that what the Lord gives to the Council, they will be able to give to the congregation—but also that whatever *he* is able to slip in will become part of the package. As the Council members come to recognize this factor of spiritual warfare, the exercise of those virtues which frustrate Satan—love, patience, long-suffering—become not a moralistic achievement which they "ought to do," but, quite simply, good battle strategy. They come to realize, then, how dependent they really are on the support and prayers of one another, and of the congregation, both for themselves and for their families.

All of this takes quite for granted, of course, the essential *ground* of our unity, which is Christ himself, as revealed in the Scripture. It deals with the practical question of how Christ can and will manifest that unity in the concrete affairs of a fellowship of believers. As the different functions of the human body are distributed, so that the eye sees, the ear hears, and the stomach receives food—each one performing its function on behalf of the whole body—so, in the Body of Christ, the various functions are distributed. Unity is a vital need for the whole Body, down to the least member. The function of *maintaining* that unity rests primarily with the Council.

CHAPTER EIGHT

Ministry in the
Body of Christ

The Catholic Apostolic Church's idea of ministry grows out of its understanding of the Church as in truth a 'body.' The ministries of the Church are the various organs of the Body of Christ, fit together and functioning according to its divinely given constitution. They draw much from the catalog of ministries which Paul lists in Ephesians 4:11, and what the Apostle then goes on to say about these ministries: "Apostles, prophets, evangelists, pastors and teachers: for the equipment of the saints, for the work of ministry, for building up the body of Christ . . . unto mature manhood." The documents of the Scottish National Church, in Irving's day, stated plainly that the extraordinary gifts of Apostle, Prophet, and Evangelist had departed from the Church.[86] The Catholic Apostolic Church reasoned: If Christ provided these ministries for bringing His body to perfection, how can we presume that it will come to perfection without them?

The "four-fold ministry," as it was called, became a foundational stone in the building of their churches. Early in the movement, men were called by the word of prophecy into the various ministries, as apostle, prophet, evangelist, pastor-teacher. While these were thought of primarily as ministers to the Church Universal, i.e., having a trans-local authority, these ministries also had counterparts in each local congregation. Each congregation, in turn, was organized under a bishop, together with elders and deacons and various 'helps.' Thus an elaborate heirarchy developed, with oftentimes complex interrelationships. One almost gets the feeling, as he studies the movement, that *everybody* was *something!*

The theological elaboration for this concept of a widely distributed ministry, and the practical delineation of each calling, is painstakingly thorough in the literature of the Catholic Apostolic Church, and, at many points, truly profound. At points one finds direct application for the Church today. But for many congregations and fellowships, the general concept itself is enough to begin a revolution. When the idea begins to take hold that 1) *I* may have a ministry to perform in this fellowship; 2) I may *receive ministry*, not only from the "pastor," but from many others as well—that may well herald the beginning of a re-vitalized church!

The problem, as we have noted, is twofold: First, the individual member must come to the conviction that he has a *ministering role* in the congregation, has something as unique to contribute to the church as each of his physical organs has to contribute to his body. Secondly, members must come to *accept the ministry which God brings them through fellow members*, who may or may not be of the ordained clergy. Of the two, we have discovered, the second is probably the greater problem. Simple, practical tasks one will accept from a layman; and certain tasks, such as teaching Sunday School, perforce could not be done otherwise. But when the need even verges on something 'spiritual,' then the pastor and only the pastor can handle it. A layman may have a proven ministry of counseling or praying for the sick, yet only slowly, and with much education, does a typical congregation come to accept that ministry as 'fully authentic.' It may be that the solemnities with which the Catholic Apostolic Church ordained even the humblest office in the church was not without point: It set before the people in an impressive manner a person to whom they could look in a time of specific need.

The idea of 'body ministry,' i.e., a ministry widely distributed throughout the membership of a church, is commonplace in the charismatic movement—in theory, if less so in practice. A breakaway from clergy domination of ministry may be one of the most significant and lasting contributions which the charismatic movement makes to the Church.

In the Catholic Apostolic Church, two elements could play into a call into some area of ministry: personal initiative, and prophetic revelation. A person might present himself, say, as a candidate for an office in the church, which in turn would be confirmed by prophecy; or, a word of prophecy might single out some individual for special ministry.

The 'volunteer method' has been the staple of the charismatic movement, from the exercise of spiritual gifts to the hum-drum ministries of service. We seem to think that direct, spontaneous inspiration is the only way the Holy Spirit operates. If someone 'feels moved' to pray for the sick, or teach Sunday School, or speak in tongues, or work in the office, or call on the unchurched in the community, why, then let him! If someone else doesn't feel so moved, then that's just the way it is. There is a sense in which this is valid: The final decision can never be taken away from the person himself. That is part of our freedom in Christ.

But how is a person *prepared* to make that final decision? Only by his own impulses, in response to such broadcast admonitions as might come in a sermon or a general announcement for volunteers? It may be that God will lead a person directly; indeed, it is usually so. But that leading often needs the catalyst of a spoken word from another person. We have just recently begun to discover how important this ministry of prophetic utterance is, in regard to *calling forth ministry*. It is not enough to exhort people to 'find their ministry.' Those called to positions of leadership must pray for the prophetic insight and pastoral wisdom to *see* the ministries which God has put within the fellowship, and, having seen them, to call them forth. It is a tremendous encouragement for a member to realize that someone else sees an anointing of God upon his life. Often, we have discovered, this revelation serves to *confirm* something the person has already seen himself—he felt drawn to a particular area of ministry, but it needed a word of confirmation and encouragement to activate it.

The corollary to this is that a word of prophecy or pastoral counsel may also be used to indicate the ministry in which a particular person should *not* serve. 'Not all are apostles, not all are prophets, not all are teachers.' Many are called to simple ministries to 'helps.' *Without these humble roles, the Body of Christ could not function.* They are absolutely essential—the humble duties and tasks that often go all but unnoticed by people (they shouldn't!), but never by God. Indeed, the Bible suggests that to these should go the greater honor (1 Cor. 12:24).

Thus, step by step, word by word, an odd-lot conglomeration of quite ordinary human beings can be fitted and joined together into a Body, a 'dwelling place for God in the Spirit.'

CHAPTER NINE

Authority in the Body of Christ

The Catholic Apostolic Church accepted the canonical Scriptures as the Church's primary authority. During their year of retreat, the apostles saw clearly that they were being entrusted with no "new Gospel," but with a restoration and illumination of the only Gospel. They saw the Scriptures as God's greatest treasure for His weak and divided Church down through the centuries. And therefore they felt bound to set forth nothing except that which was taken from the Bible, or stood in clear agreement with it.[87]

Yet, having taken that essentially Protestant position, the apostles realized that they had not dealt adequately with the question of authority. The innumerable divisions of Protestantism have all gone away from each other to set up separate housekeeping with Bibles clutched firmly in hand. An individual—or a church—may say, "The

Bible is my only authority." But what is really being said is this: "My authority is *what I understand the Bible to say.*" One cannot escape the subjective judgments which are involved in interpreting the Bible.

It is not quite accurate to score Protestants for having a 'paper pope.' What Protestants really have is a whole collection of flesh-and-blood popes—from the pastor of a local church, who solemnly declares to his vestry meeting that "This is what the Bible says to us . . . "; to the delegates at a national church convention, who decide by majority vote what the Bible says to a specific situation; to the theological professor who rests his case on the "proven results of scientific scholarship"; to the spunky layman who takes Luther at his word, and decides that he is greater than emperor, popes, or councils. The sheer proliferation of Protestant sects over the centuries is mute testimony to the fact that the Bible—which calls Christians to a real, and not merely a theoretical unity—in and of itself is not the instrument which will bring about that unity. Protestants, so long and so thoroughly convinced that the Roman Catholic Church did not have the right answer with its office of an infallible pope, have watched with interest, and perhaps a touch of unholy glee, as the Catholic Church has begun to call into question the principle of infallibility. But as yet, not many have recognized the Protestant plight in regard to a center of authority as clearly as Lutheran theologian George Lindbeck. In regard to removing the principle of infallibility from the office of authority, he says: "One metaphor which could be used in describing the infallibility debate is that it is concerned with how to extract a tumorous growth from a vital organ without committing suicide. This is not a condescending comparison (for Protestants to use). The Protestant is well aware that *his* churches lack the vital organ in question." [88]

The 'vital organ in question,' according to the Catholic Apostolic Church, is the college of Apostles. It is in acting through them, as His *chief organ of authority*, that Christ means to maintain His Church in unity, and reveal to her the truth. It inheres in the very nature of the Apostolate, by virtue of its direct appointment from Christ, that final authority in the Church, humanly speaking, rests here.[89]

In terms of formal structure, what we have in the Catholic Apostolic Church is an oligarchy, 'the rule of the few.' It distinguishes from the formal autocracy of the Roman Catholic Church on the one hand,

and from the alleged democracy of Protestantism on the other. Seen purely in terms of formal structure, it has a strong authoritarian coloring.

One must see this authority working 'from the inside,' however, in order to grasp its real nature. While the Catholic Apostolic Church had a high regard for authority, a crass authoritarianism was utterly foreign to its spirit. They recognized that the secret of spiritual power and authority lay not in human position or capability, but paradoxically, in weakness. "When I am weak, then I am strong" (2 Cor. 12:9).

On July 14, 1835, when the apostles were set apart in a great festival celebration, the bishops of the seven churches in London were addressed in prophecy: "The spiritual babe is given into your keeping . . . the Twelve in their weakness, as a child." [90] A strange inaugural for men called to the highest position of leadership in a church, yet quite in keeping with Catholic Apostolic thought. As leaders, they were to exemplify for the people the basic human condition upon which the authority and power of the Church depends, a sense of weakness and childlike dependency on God. The people, though they held their leaders in high regard, were taught to look continually to

God for the restoration of the Church.[91] The first outbreak of spiritual gifts, through a simple, uneducated country girl lying on her deathbed,[92] was in fact a graphic paradigm for t h e Catholic Apostolic Church, as she sought for the restoration of apostolic power and order. The apostles, in common with all believers, must beseech God *out of their weakness* for the power and authority to accomplish their task.[93]

Thus in the Catholic Apostolic Church we see the paradox of an outward form which lays great stress upon title, position, authority, and honor; yet an inner life in which all human authority is subordinated to, and ultimately verified by, the call and the working of the Holy Spirit.

The Catholic Apostolic Church saw no contradiction between charismatic authority and formal heirarchical structure, an instructive parallel to sub-apostolic times, where "the co-existence of these various kinds of authority is not felt to be a problem."[94] Indeed, the Catholic Apostolic Church believed that the structure was as much a gift and revelation of God as was the charismatic power. The rule of the apostles over the churches, the rule of bishop and elders over the flock, the rule of father over the family they held to be part of a divinely revealed order through which the authority of Christ manifests itself most effectively.

In order to grasp the Catholic Apostolic Church's understanding of authority and order, we must perhaps disenthrall ourselves from a certain amount of popular prejudice. The idea of participatory democracy has become so much a part of the structure of our thinking, that it is exceedingly difficult for us to appreciate another kind of order, in which democratic proceedings, as such, would play a more limited role. Yet it may be, as C. S. Lewis has pointed out, that the very spread of democracy in the political sphere will accentuate the need for other kinds of order in the churches.

"I believe in political equality," writes Lewis. "But there are two opposite reasons for being a democrat. You may think all men so good that they deserve a share in the government of the commonwealth, and so wise that the commonwealth needs their advice. That is, in my opinion, the false, romantic doctrine of democracy. On the other hand, you may believe fallen men to be so wicked that not one of them can be trusted with any irresponsible power over his fellows. That I believe to be the true ground of democracy. I do not believe that God created an egalitarian world. I believe the authority of parent over child, husband over wife, learned over simple, to have been as much a part of the original plan as the authority of man over beast. I believe that if we had not fallen Filmer would be right, and patriarchal monarchy would be the sole lawful government. But since we have learned sin, we have found, as Lord Acton says, that 'all power corrupts, and absolute power corrupts absolutely.' The only remedy has been to take away the powers and substitute a legal fiction of equality... Do not misunderstand me. I am not in the least belittling the value of this egalitarian fiction, which is our only defense against one another's cruelty. But the function of equality is purely protective. It is medicine, not food. By treating human persons as if they were all the same kind of thing, we avoid innumerable evils. But it is not on this that we were made to live... Authority exercised with humility and obedience accepted with delight are the very lines along which our spirits live. Even in the life of the affections, much more in the Body of Christ, we step outside that world which says 'I am as good as you.' It is like turning from a march to a dance. We become, as Chesterton said, taller when we bow; we become lowlier when we instruct. It delights me that there should be moments in the services of my own Church when the priest stands and I kneel. As democracy becomes more complete in the outer world and opportunities for reverence are successively removed, the refreshment, the cleansing, and invigorating returns to inequality which the Church offers us, become more and more necessary." [95]

Perhaps the time has come for someone to say a good word for 'authority,' and even for 'authoritarianism,' rightly understood. Our culture has developed an almost Pavlovian response; we come up frothing at the mere mention of the words. And not altogether without cause. Our age has suffered through some frightening abuses of authoritarian power. Yet we need to ask ourselves whether reaction against bad authoritarianism validates a rejection of the authoritarian in our culture *per se*, if indeed that were possible.

What would happen to our culture if we were suddenly robbed of the legacy which we have received from men of authoritarian stature? To this day, the authoritarian figure of Moses towers over the Judeo-Christian heritage. In the New Testament, the Apostle Paul did not shy away from speaking to the Corinthians in strong authoritarian tones, threatening to come to them 'with a rod.' Again and again, in the writings of the Apostles, the note of unquestioned authority is sounded. Indeed, throughout the Bible this is to be seen. God himself is the quintessence of the benevolent authoritarian Father; and those whom He calls to administer His business express themselves in authoritarian terms.

One writer has said that Abraham Lincoln was among the most authoritarian of American presidents, because of the way he aggrandized power to the office of president. What would the United States be today had it not been for the kind of leadership which he offered at the juncture of history? The Roman Catholic Church today, in the throes of great change, finds that it cannot call into question the authoritarian stance of the Church without real anguish, because that very stance has been the source of no small measure of blessing and strength down through the centuries.

Some might propose a semantic solution to the problem, distinguishing between 'authority' and 'authoritarian,' and this is not without point. But it runs the risk of obscuring a factor we need to face up to: That throughout history men of authoritarian stature have risen up and left a significant and positive legacy to mankind. It may

101

be that men of authoritarian stature are an intrinsic and inevitable part of history and of society. Perhaps we do not have the choice between anti-authoritarian and authoritarian, but, hopefully, between good and bad authoritarians. It at least gives one pause to think, when we note that the counter-culture in the United States, ostensibly anti-authoritarian, chooses Mao-tze Tung for one of its folk heroes.

In the Catholic Apostolic Church, both family and church were structured along authoritarian lines. The position of authority was conceived of primarily as a place from which to serve. The right and need to rule grew out of the responsibility for serving. The practical exercise of authority was therefore by no means rigid and unilateral. Within one's proper sphere, a person exercised authority which those over him were bound to respect. Thus "bishops, though under the authority of the apostles, yet have the authority to 'try all who desire to exercise the apostolic office, and admit or reject them' (after the analogy of *Revelation 2:2*) . . . they alone, and not the apostles, are wedded to their churches by the act of consecration, as a man is wedded to his wife. Although they are not ministers of the Universal Church, and have not so extended a jurisdiction, yet they are of higher rank in another sense, as performing higher and more spiritual functions. The leading on of every individual in the paths of holiness belongs to them, and not to the ministers of the Universal Church." [96]

The fact that one may, in a particular situation, serve another from a position of authority does not mean that the authority extends automatically into other areas. "Bishops receive strength from the imposition of apostles' hands to fulfill their independent duties ... so do husbands receive the imposition of bishops' hands to be confirmed or strengthened in that measure of the Holy Ghost which is necessary for them to exercise their duties; and as no apostle may interfere in the private administration of the affairs of a church, neither may the pastor of a parish flock interfere in the private administration of the affairs of a family." [97]

This same regard for spheres of authority is recognized within the structure of the family: "Everyone has an inclination to shine in that which is not within his border, and to show his wisdom where no charge has been committed to him. Into this error the woman falls, who is eager to put in her word with her husband in his higher duties. Into this error the man falls when he mixes himself up with all

103

the matters of housekeeping, and fancies that he understands them better than his wife." [98] The practical exercise of authority is thus highly *functional*. In the sphere where one ministers, he exercises a corresponding authority which is regarded by all, those over him and those under him. Within the patriarchal structure of the Catholic Apostolic Church there thus developed a high degree of *mutuality*.

The Catholic Apostolic Church early recognized that charismatic power cannot exist apart from strong spiritual authority. The 'gifts' and the 'offices' stand in integral relation with one another. "Where apostolic authority is lacking or not recognized, the spiritual gifts can not come to full power and maturity; they will be stunted by disorder and excesses." [99] When people involved in the charismatic movement come to see this, they will be able to relate much more positively to their church structures—seeing in them not a threat to their new-found spiritual life, but a necessary counterpoise.

This is even true where the church authority may not be altogether sympathetic with the charismatic experience. It is tempting to dismiss church authorities who disagree as 'unspiritual,' and go off to find one's own 'authority,' some person or group which approves of the charismatic experience. Self-chosen authorities are rarely God-appointed authorities. The essence of authority is that one is *placed* under them, by God. It is usually safest to begin right where one is, accepting one's family structure and church structure as God's appointed place. Christians do not grow only by getting 'fed,' by having wonderful prayer meetings, Bible studies, and fellowship, important as these are. They also grow through the adversities which they suffer, including fellow Christians, even pastor or priest, who are less than helpful or sympathetic in a given situation. When a situation is recognized and accepted as part of God's plan, it casts it in an altogether different light— not something to run away from, but something to learn from.

The question of authority haunts the charismatic movement. How does, how can, the freedom of the Spirit relate in a wholesome way to the order and authority of the Church? Indeed, this is a question which movements of renewal have had to face through the centuries, and all too seldom has a renewal movement and the Church arrived at a satisfactory *detente*. One man has expressed the gist of the problem in a memorable way: "Historically, the 'heirarchy,' the officialdom of the

Church, has tended to suppress the gifts *of the Holy Spirit* (1 Corinthians 12:4-11); they bid well to upset the *status quo*, threaten the smooth functioning of the ecclesiastical machinery. But what is less often recognized is the tendency of renewal movements to reject the gifts *of Christ* (Ephesians 4:11)—those ministries of *authority* which are given to bring the Church to maturity." [100]

Arising in protest against spiritual lethargy in the Church, revivals often look warily at anything that smacks of 'order' or 'office' as the sure corollary to spiritual death; it seems to threaten the new-found life in the renewal movement. Yet both are essential. Without the gifts of the Holy Spirit freely manifested through a many-membered Body, the Church can all too easily become a museum piece. But without the Christ-ordained ministries of authority, without Spirit-given structures to direct and shepherd the life, the fire of the Spirit can too easily become wild fire, and burn itself out in a short display of spiritual pyrotechnics.

It must be honestly recognized that this tendency toward spiritual anarchy has not been absent from the charismatic movement. Anarchy is not God's way. It is impossible for the work of the Spirit to be separated from the exercise of God-appointed spiritual authority. History provides ample illustration of awakening movements which have developed their own forms of order and authority, and in astonishingly short periods of time have become as rigid and calcified as those against whom they originally protested. The charismatic movement, if it is to remain spiritually healthy—if it is to be of ultimate blessing to the Church—if it is to fulfill God's plan and purpose—must look long and hard at the whole question of spiritual authority.

CHAPTER TEN

"Unless a Seed Fall into the Ground and Die . . ."

It remains now only to note the historical ebb of the Catholic Apostolic Church, and the reasons for it. The first apostle died in 1855,[101] portending a slow dying out of the Catholic Apostolic Church itself, for according to their order, only Apostles could ordain to the priesthood, and only ordained priests could celebrate the Eucharist.

One by one the apostles passed on, until at the turn of the century only one remained alive. In Germany, some attempts were made to perpetuate the movement by calling new apostles, but these were never recognized; they formed a splinter group which became known as the New Apostolic Church. The Catholic Apostolic Church itself registered no qualms as the end of their Work loomed on the horizon. Already in the early days of the movement, the prophecies had indicated that, in the Spirit, this Work must experience all Christ's sufferings, and then die with Him.[102]

Yet in that very expectation of death, there was a new hope. For several decades there had been prophecies concerning the "Mission of the 70"—a second, and greater Work, which God would raise up in due time. Theirs was the "Mission of the 12," corresponding to Jesus' appointment of the Twelve Apostles near the beginning of His ministry; the new Work would correspond to the appointment of the 70 (Luke 10:1), near the end of His ministry.[103] If their Work were to end as a seed, dropped into the ground to die, then God, in His own time and way, would bring forth new life. Nor did they fret that their Work, which they believed to be so freighted with divine purpose, was but little recognized in Christendom. From early days, there had been prophecies that it was to be a "hidden work" of God.[104]

The last of the apostles died in 1901, and the Catholic Apostolic Church entered its period of silence. Service and ministry continued while ordained priests remained alive, but gradually these too passed on. Asked by a sympathetic outsider what they would do when the last priest died, a member said, "The proof of the genuineness of our claim to be raised up, not as a sect,

109

but a Church within the Church, to await
the coming of the Bridegroom, lies in our
dependence on His will. We make no
plans." [105]

One ordained priest, well past 90, remains alive, in England. Only there may
the full Eucharistic Service be celebrated.
Elsewhere the altars are covered. Thus
with quiet dignity the Catholic Apostolic
Church resigns itself to the inscrutable
mystery of God's Providence.

The Catholic Apostolic Church seemed
to take but little note of the Pentecostal
movement, when it burst upon the scene
in the early years of the century. Perhaps
the worship and order were too strange,
too lacking in form, for them to feel a
sense of kinship with it. But when the charismatic movement surfaced in the early
1960's, it wakened keen interest among a
number of people with roots in the Catholic
Apostolic Church. They scrutinized the
movement carefully, and went back to the
prophecies concerning "the 70," a second
great work which God would initiate to
bring about the restoration of His Church.

Catholic Apostolic people recognize that
the Church needs the charismatic, that it
offers to the Church a fresh outpouring of
the Holy Spirit. But they also recognize—
and this is the essence of their message

110

to the charismatic movement—that *the charismatic needs the Church*. God does not give a new outpouring of the Holy Spirit for the private pleasure and blessing of individuals; that is purely a by-product. The Holy Spirit comes to glorify Christ, to build up His Body. Central to that ministry of the Holy Spirit are the offices of spiritual authority which are given "for the equipment of the saints, for the work of ministry, for building up the body of Christ" (Eph. 4:12). The 'gifts of Christ'— those men invested with offices of spiritual authority in the Church—are meant to oversee and guide the members as they manifest the various gifts of the Holy Spirit. The bestowal of a gift of the Holy Spirit does not necessarily carry with it the corresponding wisdom to manifest and use that gift in the most profitable way. That wisdom is more to be found in the 'gifts of Christ'—those men whom He gives to His Church that she might be built up and prepared for His return.

Over the years, Catholic Apostolic people have learned to speak of "the Lord's Work" with great reserve, even enigmatically. But when one gains the confidence of some of them, now well advanced in years, who still recall as yesterday the rich worship, and the life of the Spirit in

111

which they were nurtured, and discusses with them the moving of God's Spirit, one has the distinct impression that he is not being told so much a recollection of what has been, as an expectation of what is yet to be.

As the charismatic movement sifts and weighs the message of the Catholic Apostolic Church, learning and putting into practice within the Church that which is of enduring worth, a seed which of set purpose fell into the ground and died, may yet bear a rich harvest for the Kingdom of God.

* * * * * * * * * *

Notes

1. Drummond A. L. *Edward Irving and His Circle*, pp. 153, 214. James Clarke and Co., Ltd., London, 1934.

Rossteuscher, Dr. Ernst Adolph. *Der Aubau der Kirche Chrisit auf den spruenglichen Grundlagen. Eine geschichtliche Darstellung seiner Anfaenge*, 244, 199, 304-5, 282-3, 335-7, 218-19, 258, 292, 302. Verlag Hermann Meier Nachf., Siegen (first printed in 1871; reprinted, 1969).

Shaw, P. E. *The Catholic Apostolic Church, Sometimes Called Irvingite, A Historical Study*, pp. 30, 36, 237. Kings Crown Press, Morningside Heights, New York, 1946.

Oliphant, Mrs. Margaret O. W. *The Life of Edward Irving*, p. 289. Hurst and Blackett, Publishers, London, 1864.

Sitwell, Francis. *The Purpose of God in Creation*, p. 204ff. Thomas Laurie, Edinburgh, 1875.

2. Strachan, Gordon, *Edward Irving and Regent Square: A Presbyterian Pentecost*, p. 15. Unpublished article by doctoral candidate at New College, Edinburgh. His reference is specifically to Edward Irving, but would apply equally to the Catholic Apostolic Church as a body.

3. Morse-Boycott, Desmond. *They Shine*

Like Stars (history of the Oxford Movement), p. 308. Skeffington and Son, Ltd., London, 1947.

4. Davenport, John Sidney. *Edward Irving and the Catholic Apostolic Church*, p. 18. John Moffet, New York, 1863.

5. Wilks, Washington. *Edward Irving: An Ecclesiastical and Literary Biography*, p. 266. William Freeman, 69 Fleet Street, London, 1854.

6. Whitley, A. C. *Blinded Eagle*, p. 78. SCM Press, Ltd., London, 1955.

7. Rossteuscher, *op. cit.*, pp. 420, 425.

8. Edel, Dr. Reiner-Friedemann. *Heinrich Thiersch als oekumenische Gestalt*, see especially pp. 89-136, 244-247, 256. Verlag Dr. R. F. Edel, Marburg an der Lahn, Germany 1962.

9. Copinger, H. B. *A Bibliography Begun Easter 1908*, mimeographed for private circulation.

10. Harper, Michael, *As at the Beginning*, p. 13. Hodder and Stoughton, London, 1965.

11. Rossteuscher, *op. cit.*, pp. 195, 199, 200.

12. Drummond, A. L., *op. cit.*, p. 153.

13. Andrews, W. W. *The History and Claims of the Body of Christians Known as the Catholic Apostolic Church*, pp. 15-16. H. B. Copinger, Wembley, Middlesex, England, 1950.

14. Abbott, Walter, M., editor. *The Documents of Vatican II*, p. 709. Guild Press, New York, 1966.

15. Brunner, Emil. *The Misunderstanding of the Church*, pp. 51-52. Lutterworth Press, London, 1954.

16. Rossteuscher, *op. cit.*, pp. 278-307.

17. *Ibid.*, p. 437.

18. Andrews, W. W. *Edward Irving: A Review*, pp. 37-38. David Hobbs & Co., Glasgow, 1900.

19. Oliphant, *op. cit.*, pp. 362-64.

20. Rossteuscher, *op. cit.*, p. 168.

21. Whitley, *op. cit.*, p. 34.

22. Drummond, A. L., *op. cit.*, p. 154.

23. Rossteuscher, *op. cit.*, pp. 273, 234.

24. *Ibid.*, pp. 244-45.

25. Whitley, *op. cit.*, p. 76.

26. Oliphant, *op. cit.*, pp. 378-79.

27. See, for example: Oliphant, *op. cit.*, pp. 389, 405; Drummond, A. L., *op. cit.*, p. 232; Rossteuscher, *op. cit.*, p. 330.

28. Strachan, *op. cit.*, p. 2.

29. Oliphant, *op. cit.*, pp. 257-67.

30. Private information.

31. Oliphant, *op. cit.*, p. 398.

32. Wilks, *op. cit.*, pp. 280-86.

33. Oliphant, *op. cit.*, p. 389.

34. Andrews, W. W. *Edward Irving etc.*, *op. cit.*, p. 166.

35. Shaw, *op. cit.*, p. 56.

36. Strachan, *op. cit.*, pp. 14, 21.

37. Andrews, W. W. *Edward Irving etc.*, *op. cit.*, p. 167.

38. Rossteuscher, *op. cit.*, p. 211.

39. *Ibid.*, p. 305.

40. *Ibid.*, p. 346; see also Shaw, *op. cit.*, p. 75.

41. Rossteuscher, *op. cit.*, pp. 346-47.

42. Woodehouse, F. W. *A Narrative of Events Affecting the Position and Prospects of the Whole Christian Church*, pp. 51-54. The Bedford

Bookshop, 10 Tavistock Place, London, 1938.

43. Rossteuscher, *op. cit.*, p. 419.

44. Armbruster, Carl and Begley, John. "Ministry, Office, and Ordination," *Worship*, October 1971, p. 464. Collegeville, Minnesota.

45. Andrews, Samuel J., *The Church and Its Organic Ministries: A Plea for the Headship of Christ*, pp. 2-6. David Hobbs & Co., Glasgow, 1899.

46. *Testimony Addressed to the Rulers in Church and State in Christian Lands*, pp. 40-41. Delivered 1837. Reprinted in 1888.

47. Cardale, John Bates. *Readings Upon the Liturgy, Volume 2*, p. 405. Thomas Bosworth, London, 1878.

48. Edel, *op. cit.*, p. 158.

49. Andrews, Samuel J., *op. cit.*, p. 37.

50. *Testimony, etc., op. cit.*, p. 65.

51. Andrews, W. W. *The History and Claims, etc., op. cit.*, pp. 7-8.

52. Rossteuscher, *op. cit.*, p. 347.

53. Edel, *op. cit.*, p. 256.

54. Shaw, *op. cit.*, pp. 237-38.

55. McDonnell, Kilian. "Ways of Validating Ministry," *Journal of Ecumenical Studies*, Spring 1970, p. 264.

56. Morse-Boycott, *op. cit.*, pp. 307, 308.

57. Edel, *op. cit.*, p. 80. See his reference to the German scholar Kurt Hutten's evaluation of the "Testimony" as "a serious document, worthy of high regard." See also Morse-Boycott, *op. cit.*, p. 307: "A supreme literary achievement, instinct with a beautiful Christian spirit, informed from depths of wisdom and redolent

with an unction equal to their claims which, we must note, were modestly put forward, without any show."

58. Woodehouse, *op. cit.*, pp. 58-59.

59. Edel, *op. cit.*, p. 199.

60. Rossteuscher, *op. cit.*, p. 368, 420-21.

61. Andrews, W. W. *The History and Claims, etc., op. cit.*, p. 46.

62. Rossteuscher, *op. cit.*, p. 465.

63. This judgment is based on a number of personal contacts which the writer has had, both with elderly members of the Catholic Apostolic Church who have shared extensively, and with other researchers who render a like judgment. See also, e.g., Shaw, *op cit.*, p. 142; Morse-Boycott, *op. cit.*, pp. 307-309.

64. Woodehouse, *op. cit.*, p. 123.

65. *Ibid.*, p. 119.

66. Drummond, A. L., *op. cit.*, p. 164.

67. Cardale, *op. cit.*, p. 291.

68. *Ibid.*, pp. 296-97.

69. *Ibid.*, p. 440.

70. Woodehouse, *op. cit.*, p. 121.

71. *Ibid.*, pp. 130-31.

72. Cardale, *op. cit.*, p. 424.

73. *Ibid.*, p. 435; and—
Andrews, Samuel J., *op. cit.*, pp. 129, 131; and—
Woodehouse, *op. cit.*, p. 127.

74. McDonnell, Kilian. Stated in a seminar, Tulsa, Oklahoma, April, 1972.

75. Woodehouse, *op. cit.*, pp. 132-33.

76. Morse-Boycott, *op. cit.*, p. 308.

77. Cardale, *op. cit.*, p. 445.

78. Williams, J. Rodman. "An Open Letter to the Editor," *Newsletters of the Charismatic Communion of Presbyterian Ministers*, 428 N.W. 34th Street, Oklahoma City, Oklahoma, 1970.

79. Bittlinger, Arnold. "Aspects of Christian Initiation," a paper given at The Institute for Ecumenical and Cultural Research, Collegeville, Minnesota, January 5, 1972.

80. Hogan, Joseph. "Charismatic Renewal in the Catholic Church: An Evaluation," *New Covenant*, September 1971, p. 2. Box 102, Main Str. Station, Ann Arbor, Michigan.

81. Shaw, *op. cit.*, p. 241.

82. Rossteuscher, *op. cit.*, pp. 506, 508.

83. Andrews, W. W. *The True Constitution of the Church; and Its Restoration*, pp. 30-31, John Moffet, 82 Nassau Street, New York, 1854.

84. Boehm, Charles J. T. *Lights and Shadows in the Present Condition of the Church*, pp. 145-46. Thomas Bosworth, London, 1874.

85. Rossteuscher, *op. cit.*, pp. 455-56.

86. *Ibid.*, p. 273.

87. *Ibid.*, p. 472.

88. Lindbeck, George, *Infallibility*, p. 2. 1972. Pere Marquette Theological Lecture, Marquette University Theology Department, Milwaukee, Wisconsin, 1972.

89. Rossteuscher, *op. cit.*, p. 348.

90. *Ibid.*, p. 465.

91. Wilks, *op. cit.*, p. 281.

92. Rossteuscher, *op. cit.*, p. 195.

93. *Ibid.*, p. 346, 350.

94. von Campenhausen, Hans. *Ecclesiastical Authority and Spiritual Power in the Church*

of the First Three Centuries, p. 178. Stanford University Press, Stanford, California, 1969.

95. Lewis, C. S. "Membership," *Transposition and Other Addresses*, pp. 39-41. Geoffrey Bles, London, 1949.

96. Drummond, Henry. *Abstract Principles of Revealed Religion*, pp. 261-63. John Murray, London, 1845.

97. *Ibid.*, p. 246-47.

98. Thiersch, H.W.J. *Christian Family Life*, pp. 62-63. Thomas Bosworth, London, 1880.

99. Rossteuscher, *op. cit.*, p. 211.

100. Godschalk, Dr. J. A leader of a renewal movement in Holland, in private conversation.

101. Shaw, *op. cit.*, p. 243.

102. Rossteuscher, *op. cit.*, p. 475.

103. Thonger, James. *Eight Sermons on "The Seventy,"* mimeographed manuscript of sermons preached by the 'Angel' of Leeds, 1887.